COUNCIL *on*
FOREIGN
R ELATIONS

Council Special Report No. 93
April 2022

Reflecting Sunlight to Reduce Climate Risk

Priorities for Research and International Cooperation

Stewart M. Patrick

CONTENTS

FOREWORD

Many people tend to think about climate change as a crisis of the future, something that often leads to the climate agenda being shunted to the side in favor of more immediate issues. And while the crisis will grow worse, it is essential to recognize that climate change is already here. It is already resulting in widespread fires, deadly floods, severe storms, serious water shortages, and countless other effects. The data is uniformly grim, revealing that the past seven years have been the hottest in recorded history. Unless the largest emitters take drastic action, the world will fail to meet the Paris Climate Agreement's goals. Last November's gathering in Glasgow mostly produced promises and pronouncements rather than meaningful, enforceable commitments. More recently, climate policy across the globe has taken a back seat to considerations of energy security linked to the crisis in Ukraine. The Joe Biden administration's decision to lift the summertime ban on sales of higher-ethanol gas, open more public land to drilling, and release a historic amount of oil from the country's strategic petroleum reserve illustrates this point. And the United States is far from alone.

Governments around the world have employed three main approaches to combat climate change. The first is emissions reductions. The Paris Climate Agreement aims to reduce global emissions in a bid to limit the global temperature increase to 2°C (3.6°F) above preindustrial levels. The United States has announced that it is seeking to reduce its greenhouse gas emissions by 50 to 52 percent compared with 2005 levels by 2030. China has pledged that its carbon dioxide emissions will peak before 2030 and it will achieve net-zero emissions before 2060. It is far from certain these goals will be met and, even if they are, that they will be sufficient. A second approach is carbon dioxide removal, which entails capturing and storing atmospheric carbon through natural or mechanical means. The promise here is likewise uncertain. A third approach, adaptation, aims to build resilience to mitigate the effects of a warmer planet. But the reality is that the first two strategies are occurring far too slowly, and adaptation, while vital, by definition seeks to contend with the worst effects of climate change rather than prevent them.

In this Council Special Report, Stewart M. Patrick, James H. Binger senior fellow and director of the International Institutions and Global Governance program at the Council on Foreign Relations, explores an additional tool to address climate change: sunlight reflection. His report is grounded in what might be described as climate realism: he sees climate change as a large and growing threat but judges (correctly in my view) that existing national and international efforts, however necessary and desirable, are not even close to being adequate.

Patrick argues correctly that the potential of sunlight reflection (until recently more commonly known as geoengineering) should be scrutinized. While the science is in its infancy, the idea is simple: to reduce the heating effect of solar radiation by reflecting the sun's rays back from the earth to block about 1 percent of incoming sunlight. Two main approaches exist. One method would entail dispersing aerosols or other particulates into the stratosphere, while the other would involve spraying salt crystals from the ocean to brighten low-lying marine clouds. Patrick argues that such action would not serve as an alternative to the three existing climate change strategies noted above but rather as a complement.

Patrick goes on to make the case that even though sunlight reflection is controversial, it has enough promise to be studied further. He calls for urgent, serious investment at the national and international levels to determine the science's potential and explore the engineering and implementation challenges. Domestically, this step would necessitate developing and funding a robust research program, holding congressional hearings on U.S. responses to climate risk, passing legislation, adopting a balanced approach to research governance, and analyzing the geopolitics of sunlight reflection.

Patrick asserts the importance of reassuring other nations of U.S. intentions and supporting mechanisms for international research collaboration that are not overly restrictive. He also calls for the development of a multilateral framework to govern any future deployment decisions, to reduce the growing risk that individual governments could seek to launch such programs unilaterally, with potentially destabilizing international consequences. He argues it is imperative that any institution-building effort designed to govern research, development, and deployment of sunlight reflection should complement and reinforce rather than compete with and undermine emissions cuts, carbon dioxide removal, and adaptation.

This Council Special Report builds a compelling case for investigating sunlight reflection as a potential element of a larger strategy. As Patrick writes, it is "incumbent on countries to assess the feasibility and wisdom of pursuing this option and the institutions required to govern its potential deployment." It is sad that such a report is necessary, but it will be even sadder still if we do not make exploring the potential of sunlight reflection an urgent priority.

Richard Haass
President
Council on Foreign Relations
April 2022

ACKNOWLEDGMENTS

During my tenure at the Council on Foreign Relations (CFR), I have had the pleasure and privilege of working alongside and learning from many thoughtful colleagues and renowned experts in our shared pursuit of innovative solutions to the planet's pressing problems. Researching and writing this Council Special Report has been the highlight of that experience. I want to express my profound gratitude to those who inspired this study and helped bring it to fruition.

My greatest debt is to Sherri Goodman, the indefatigable chair of my advisory committee, who has devoted her career to placing climate change and other ecological concerns at the heart of U.S. foreign and national security policy. Sherri presided over a dream team of two dozen experts spanning the worlds of atmospheric and climate science, environmental cooperation, international finance, global ethics, international law, multilateral diplomacy, policy advocacy, political science, and venture capital. While the resulting report is solely my responsibility, their generous guidance and incisive comments improved its accuracy and quality immeasurably.

At CFR, my deepest thanks go to Ania Zolyniak, a talented and tireless research associate, who scoured the relevant literature, tidied my clumsy prose, and kept me on schedule and in good spirits over innumerable Zoom sessions. Terry Mullan, my resourceful assistant director, provided additional advice. I'm also grateful to Patricia Dorff and Marcelo Agudo of CFR's Publications team for their sharp edits and rapid turnaround, and to CFR Digital's Will Merrow for producing the figures for the report. Finally, I thank CFR President Richard Haass and Director of Studies James M. Lindsay for supporting this project from its inception and pressing me to frame this technical subject in a manner that would appeal to foreign policy generalists.

The report has also benefited from conversations with Joseph Aldy, Larry Birenbaum, David Hawkins, David Keith, Nathaniel Keohane, Jane Long, Billy Pizer, Rachel Pritzker, David Schwartz, Michael Thompson, Andrew Verhalen, and Alex Wong, as well as consultations with senior U.S. government officials, the transnational Degrees Initiative network, and CFR senior fellows. Finally, I would like to thank the Robina Foundation for its generous programmatic support.

Of the many challenges confronting our world, climate change is the most daunting, threatening the integrity of the biosphere and the ecological foundations of human civilization. My hope is that this report will help persuade policymakers and the public of the need for more research on the feasibility and wisdom of sunlight reflection and the requirements for its effective international governance. If it succeeds in its intended effect, those listed here will deserve much of the credit.

Stewart M. Patrick

INTRODUCTION

The growing likelihood that the world will fail to meet the Paris Climate Agreement's temperature target and cross critical tipping points in the earth system, thus catalyzing devastating consequences for humanity, necessitates a broader portfolio of strategies to manage climate risk. This portfolio currently includes three main approaches: emissions reductions, carbon dioxide removal (CDR), and adaptation. Given the quickening pace and growing magnitude of the climate emergency, the United States and other countries should consider adding a fourth approach: sunlight reflection, which entails reflecting a small percentage of sunlight back into space to counteract its warming effect on greenhouse gases (GHGs).

The potential value of sunlight reflection—also known as solar geoengineering and solar climate intervention (SCI)—is high.[1] It offers a technologically plausible, potentially rapid, and relatively inexpensive way to slow or even reverse the rise in global temperatures caused by climate change, possibly reducing the hazards associated with dramatic warming while nations and international bodies make steady progress on the massive, protracted tasks of decarbonizing the world economy and stabilizing (and ultimately reducing) atmospheric GHG concentrations. It thus deserves genuine consideration by policymakers as another arrow in the quiver of climate risk–management strategies, alongside and supplementary to emissions cuts, CDR, and adaptation. Indeed, given the stakes, it would be irresponsible for national leaders *not* to evaluate the viability and possible consequences of SCI.

Nevertheless, critics have raised several practical objections to and ethical qualms about the prospect of sunlight reflection.[2] While these concerns merit scrutiny and assessment, danger is always relative.

Potential risks need to be evaluated and weighed not in isolation but in the context of the known hazards that humanity is *already* courting by continuing to pump vast quantities of GHGs into the atmosphere. The question is how the anticipated threats to human safety and well-being posed by climate change compare with those presented by climate change plus sunlight reflection. In other words, would the world be worse or better off were it to add sunlight reflection to its mix of climate responses?

Unfortunately, the world is not yet in a position to answer that question, given critical basic knowledge gaps about the potential efficacy and repercussions of such interventions and a paucity of norms or rules governing the intentional manipulation of Earth's climate system. Indeed, governments have been reluctant even to discuss the issue openly.[3] This situation is untenable; to confront a future of dramatic warming, humanity needs to consider *all* its options. Concomitantly, sunlight reflection involves techniques that carry risks of unintended consequences—dangers that could be magnified by uncoordinated and independent development and use.

Governments thus need a vastly improved scientific understanding of the feasibility and effects of sunlight reflection to make informed and responsible choices regarding its application. They also need an anticipatory international framework to govern any deployment decision, so that they do not find themselves scrambling and divided without agreed rules and procedures in some future moment of crisis.

With these imperatives in mind, the United States should do two things. First, it should launch a robust transdisciplinary national program on the science of sunlight reflection, grounded in international cooperation, to facilitate evidence-based decision-making. The White House should coordinate this government-wide research effort, working with Congress to expand the authorities and funding of relevant U.S. agencies and with foreign partners to create an open, collaborative research environment. Second, the United States should simultaneously catalyze collaborative international governance arrangements so that nations can jointly assess the desirability of sunlight reflection and take collective decisions on its future (non)deployment.[4] No such multilateral framework currently exists, increasing the risk that countries, individually or in small groups, could someday take unilateral actions with global consequences. The time for such investments in research and rules is now, while the science of sunlight reflection remains relatively speculative and its governance immature, even as the perils of climate change quicken and intensify.[5]

THE LIMITS OF EXISTING CLIMATE STRATEGIES

Due to high and rising atmospheric GHG concentrations, the world is poised to experience catastrophic warming, with governments needing to consider potential options for avoiding this fate. The world currently has three main strategies for managing climate risks. The first is reducing emissions. The second is carbon dioxide (CO_2) removal—or capturing and storing atmospheric carbon through natural or mechanical means.[6] The third is adaptation—or building resilience to minimize the worst effects of a warming planet.

Unfortunately, at their current paces, both emissions abatement and CDR deployment are occurring far too slowly to avert a dangerous rise in global temperatures. Adaptation—while essential—will nevertheless fail to prevent enormous human misery. Indeed, its limits will become ever more apparent as temperatures rise.[7]

The ultimate solution to the climate emergency is a combination of deep decarbonization and the removal of GHGs from the atmosphere at massive scale. Alas, the world is nowhere near where it needs to be on either front.[8] As a result of human activity, atmospheric CO_2 concentrations have risen from 280 parts per million (ppm) in 1750 to 419 ppm today—higher than at any point in at least the last three million years. The vast bulk of this increase has occurred since 1960 (see figure 1).[9] Even if carbon neutrality is achieved in the coming decades, this accumulated stock of CO_2 will remain in the atmosphere for thousands of years, locking in higher global temperatures for the foreseeable future (absent CDR).[10]

In 2015, the parties to the UN Framework Convention on Climate Change (UNFCCC), meeting in Paris, committed to hold the rise in average global temperatures to well below 2°C (3.6°F) and, if possible,

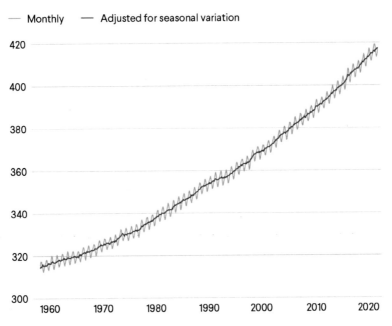

Figure 1. Rising Atmospheric Concentrations of CO_2 Since 1958

Atmospheric CO_2 at Mauna Loa Observatory (parts per million)

— Monthly   — Adjusted for seasonal variation

Sources: Scripps Institution of Oceanography; National Oceanic and Atmospheric Administration (NOAA) Global Monitoring Laboratory.

to no more than 1.5°C (2.7°F) above preindustrial levels. Today the world is poised to overshoot both these goals—badly. Humans have reduced the carbon intensity of many economic activities, but overall CO_2 emissions have not yet peaked. Last November, as the twenty-sixth Conference of the Parties (COP26) to the UNFCCC began in Glasgow, the UN Environment Program (UNEP) estimated that global emissions would need to decline by 55 percent from 2005 levels by 2030 to meet the 1.5°C Paris goal.[11] Unfortunately, before the conference, emissions were on track to rise by 16.3 percent, portending a 2.7°C (4.9°F) increase in global temperatures.[12] While new pledges made at Glasgow could—if fully met—limit warming to *just* 1.8°C (3.2°F), many of these commitments are soft and indeed implausible.[13] Moreover, those projections represent only about 66.7 percent probability outcomes; there remains a one-in-three chance that actual warming levels will be higher even if the world fulfills the Glasgow pledges (see figure 2).[14]

Figure 2. 2100 Warming Projections

Global greenhouse gas emissions under different policy scenarios (GtCO$_2$ equivalent per year)

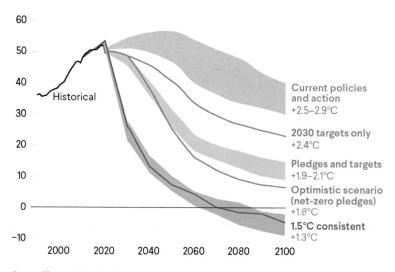

Current policies and action +2.5–2.9°C

2030 targets only +2.4°C

Pledges and targets +1.9–2.1°C

Optimistic scenario (net-zero pledges) +1.8°C

1.5°C consistent +1.3°C

Source: Climate Action Tracker.

Given the slow pace of emissions abatement, two other strategies to manage climate risk remain. The first is CDR, sucking CO$_2$ directly from the atmosphere and permanently storing it, which can be accomplished using nature-based solutions or negative emissions technologies (NETs). The former seek to enhance the world's carbon sinks by, for instance, planting trees, cultivating seaweed, increasing the health of agricultural soils, fertilizing the oceans to increase phytoplankton growth, and restoring rain, boreal, and mangrove forests.[15] The latter would encompass building machines to capture atmospheric CO$_2$ and transform it into other compounds or store it permanently underground.[16]

Both forms of CDR face significant obstacles. Implementing the necessary conservation policies and land-use changes for nature-based solutions could require decades of costly adjustments, whereas the risks of climate change are imminent. Similarly, while the pace of NET innovation is quickening, it could take half a century to bring these technologies to scale. Scientists estimate that returning atmospheric CO$_2$ concentrations to preindustrial conditions would entail removing the equivalent of thirty cubic miles of solid black carbon—a volume roughly comparable in size to Mount Rainier and a feat that would presumably dwarf any infrastructure investment ever made.[17]

The remaining currently employed strategy is adaptation, or efforts to anticipate and build resilience against the worst effects of global warming so that humanity can survive the long transition to a post-carbon economy. The coming decades will be ones of planetary upheaval and immense suffering, with more frequent and intense heat waves, storms, droughts, wildfires, sea level rise, and food insecurity. Nations and communities can ameliorate some of these calamities by adopting protective measures such as building seawalls, shifting to drought-resistant agriculture, and greening urban areas. The pace of adaptation can and should accelerate now. Nevertheless, these are essentially palliative measures to reduce—not prevent—pain and misery on a warming planet, the brunt of which will fall heaviest on the most vulnerable populations. Adaptation, moreover, is both astronomically expensive and deeply imperfect. Many nations will lack the capacity and resources to adapt, and numerous climate effects cannot be avoided: they will simply need to be borne.[18]

In short, the world confronts a high-stakes timing predicament. Although efforts to decarbonize have begun in many countries, global emissions continue to rise. The shift to renewable energy and NETs is happening far too slowly to prevent significant warming by midcentury, and adaptation has its own limitations. In this context, a fourth, potentially fast-acting, low-cost, and high-leverage way to limit increasing global temperatures and their attendant effects offers a tempting bridging option. That method is sunlight reflection.

THE LOGIC OF
SUNLIGHT REFLECTION

The idea of reflecting sunlight to reduce heat in the earth system has existed since the 1960s, but it did not attract serious consideration until 2006, when Nobel Prize laureate Paul Crutzen published an influential article on the topic.[19] The leading methods proposed to enhance Earth's reflectiveness are the stratospheric dispersal of aerosols (solid or liquid particles suspended in air) and the brightening of low-lying marine clouds.

Often relegated to science fiction, such intervention has gained plausibility thanks to advances in atmospheric research and computer modeling. Scientific observations and models suggest that it could be feasible to reduce, stop, and even reverse many effects of existing (and future) stocks of GHG emissions by reflecting the sun's rays back from Earth.[20] Such an intervention would need to block only about 1 percent of incoming sunlight to eliminate the entire temperature effects of current anthropogenic atmospheric GHGs.[21]

Recognizing the promise of sunlight reflection, the Intergovernmental Panel on Climate Change (IPCC) mentioned SCI in its 2018 special report as one method with a very high chance of keeping the increase in global temperatures below 1.5°C.[22] It thus warrants thorough study as a potential complementary approach to the climate risk–management strategies currently being applied (see table 1).[23]

Importantly, sunlight reflection is not a *solution* to climate change but rather a stopgap strategy to "shave the peak" of anticipated warming and its effects, buying time for more durable solutions to manifest and scale up (see figure 3).[24]

While SCI could in principle be done in a variety of ways, two approaches stand out. The simplest and most cost-effective method would be dispersing aerosols such as sulfur, calcite, or other particulates

Table 1. *Four Strategies for Managing Climate Risk*

Addressing underlying causes of climate change

Emissions abatement	Carbon dioxide removal (CDR)
Reduce emissions of CO_2, other GHGs, and short-lived pollutants responsible for warming through lower consumption of fossil fuels, greater energy efficiency, and adoption of renewable/clean energy sources	Remove and permanently sequester atmospheric CO_2 through a combination of nature-based solutions (e.g., reforestation) and negative emissions technologies, or NETs (e.g., direct air capture and storage)
Hurdles: Pace too slow to avoid catastrophic warming, hard to enforce commitments	*Hurdles: Could take decades to bring NETs and nature-based solutions to needed scale, and the latter present land-use trade-offs*

Surviving climate overshoot during the transition to a post-carbon economy

Adaptation	Sunlight reflection
Improve the resilience of human communities to the effects of high heat, extreme weather, changing precipitation, sea level rise, and other climate change effects	Reduce the heating effect of solar radiation by increasing Earth's albedo, particularly by dispersing aerosols in the stratosphere or brightening marine clouds
Hurdles: Targets symptoms rather than causes, is enormously expensive, and fails to avert tremendous human suffering	*Hurdles: Scientific uncertainty about efficacy, as well as relative risks vs. climate change; targets symptoms, not causes; no significant effect on GHG concentrations*

in the stratosphere either directly or in the form of precursor gases.[25] Stratospheric aerosol injection (SAI), as this technique is known, would (if using sulfur) mimic the effects of volcanic eruptions that have periodically blocked sunlight and cooled the planet, such as the eruption of Mount Pinatubo in 1991, which temporarily reduced global temperatures by about 0.6°C (1.1°F) over the following fifteen months.[26]

The most straightforward SAI method would involve dispersing reflective particles from a few dozen customized airplanes cycling continuously through the stratosphere, the second layer of Earth's atmosphere.[27] Engineers calculate that doing so would cost less than $20 billion annually, a tiny fraction of the estimated cumulative

Figure 3. Sunlight Reflection's Potential to Reduce Warming and Associated Effects

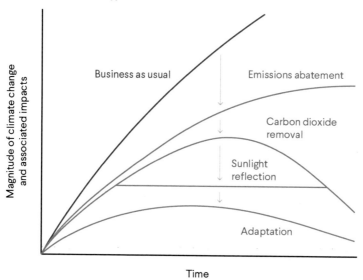

Sources: MacMartin, Ricke, and Keith, "Solar Geoengineering as Part of an Overall Strategy"; Reynolds, "Solar Geoengineering to Reduce Climate Change"; Long and Shepherd, "The Strategic Value of Geoengineering Research."

$275 trillion expense of decarbonizing the global economy by 2050.[28] To maintain the desired cooling effect, however, such injections would have to be sustained as long as atmospheric buildup of carbon dioxide and other GHGs continues.

That said, the world is already reflecting a significant amount of sunlight, albeit inadvertently and at high cost to human health, as a by-product of economic activity. Each year, the planet's nearly eight billion inhabitants send more than 250 million metric tons of particulate pollution into the atmosphere—killing at least eight million people in the process.[29] Scientists estimate that without these fine particles blunting some of the incoming solar radiation, average global temperatures would be between 0.5 and 1.1°C (0.9 and 2°F) higher than they are today, adding to the 1.1°C of heating Earth has already experienced since 1900.[30] SAI could have a similar effect with fewer health repercussions.

The second, frequently discussed technique for reflecting sunlight is marine cloud brightening (MCB), which would involve spraying salt crystals from the ocean into low-lying clouds, notionally from vessels or platforms specially designed for this purpose. It would require initially lofting particles only a few hundred feet into the air and relying on atmospheric processes to lift them higher.[31] MCB would simulate a phenomenon already visible from satellites: the generation of "ship tracks," which occur when particulate pollution from ocean vessels causes clouds above them to brighten.[32] Although sunlight reflection would be confined to certain locations, modeling shows that its temperature effects would be global.[33]

While computer models and simulations suggest that both SAI and MCB could cool Earth's climate, significant scientific uncertainties persist regarding how these methods could be implemented most effectively, and how much reflectivity they could achieve. Resolving these process-level questions will require limited, controlled field experiments. In summer 2021, Harvard University researchers, aiming to improve SAI models, planned to test delivery equipment in Sweden that in future small-scale experiments could release a tiny plume of material (about one kilogram) roughly twenty kilometers (twelve miles) into the atmosphere. Designated the Stratospheric Controlled Perturbation Experiment, the project was canceled due to protests from environmentalists, advocates for the Saami peoples of Lapland, and other activists, even though it would have had no direct consequences for either environmental or human health.[34] The first field trial of MCB was conducted in Australia in 2020 to see if MCB could reduce heat stress on the Great Barrier Reef—with promising results.[35] Current aspirations are to test an MCB spray system off the U.S. West Coast later in 2022 and to launch a small-scale MCB experiment there as early as 2023.[36]

COMMON CRITIQUES AND COMPARATIVE RISK ASSESSMENT

Despite its potential, sunlight reflection is controversial. Critics have raised a host of objections, some legitimate and reasonable and others alarmist and unpersuasive.[37] To some detractors, the notion of consciously intervening in Earth's climate system induces cosmological queasiness, because it is perceived as "playing God" in a way that is somehow different from large-scale, unintentional human influence on the earth system. Do humans even have a right to do this?[38]

Other critics fear that SCI could create a moral hazard by reducing pressure on governments, companies, and consumers to lower GHG emissions. Others are concerned that sunlight reflection, despite being hailed as "cheap," could carry tangible nonmonetary costs.[39] They worry that it could disrupt critical components of the planetary environment, such as the stratospheric ozone layer and regional precipitation patterns; affect agricultural productivity or solar power by reducing direct sunlight; endanger human health by exposing people to fine particulates; and impose an aesthetic toll in the form of slightly whiter skies and even fewer starry nights. Because it would do nothing to stop the continued accumulation of CO_2, ocean acidification would continue apace.

Skeptics also fret that SCI efforts could lack democratic accountability and legitimacy, collide with international law, and exacerbate diplomatic tensions and geopolitical rivalry as nations disagree over the merits or details of climate intervention and seek to unilaterally deploy or even weaponize it. Finally, they complain that SCI would violate principles of procedural, distributional, and intergenerational justice by permitting a select few countries to set the global thermostat, benefitting some populations and regions at others' expense, and consigning future generations to SCI schemes in perpetuity.[40] Indeed, because GHGs will continue to accumulate until a combination of emissions reductions and CDR returns GHG concentrations to preintervention levels, which could take decades, such interventions would need to persist. Were interventions to suddenly cease and not be resumed, temperatures would quickly soar. Collectively, such concerns help explain why many (though not all) environmental advocates have opposed considering sunlight reflection and why governments themselves have been reticent to act on this agenda.[41]

Some critics even object to sunlight reflection research itself, convinced that slippery slope dynamics and the "locking-in" of certain technologies (simply due to their use and development) will inevitably lead to deployment.[42] In January 2022, sixty-three prominent scholars published an open letter calling for an "international nonuse agreement on solar geoengineering," including a ban on any publicly funded research and development of relevant technologies, as well as all outdoor experiments.[43] Their stated objective was "to prevent the normalization of solar geoengineering as a climate policy option."[44]

Such a ban, however, would set a terrible precedent, chilling free scientific inquiry and rational debate. An effective taboo on such research risks depriving the world of the knowledge base to make calculated assessments and decisions concerning the feasibility, trade-offs, and repercussions of different policy options. It would also be unlikely to prevent unilateral development and deployment of sunlight reflection technologies, without necessary global safeguards, by a desperate and determined government.[45]

The potential perils of sunlight reflection merit careful evaluation because SCI is an untested enterprise susceptible to human error and unintended consequences. Moreover, even if such interventions were to reduce or even reverse temperature rise, they would not restore Earth's climate to its original state. This is because sunlight reflection seeks to offset the atmospheric heating effect of GHGs, which trap outgoing longwave radiation from Earth, not by reducing those gases but by reflecting incoming sunlight to cool the surface of the planet. It is thus an imperfect, if potentially unavoidable, response to climate change.[46]

At the same time, the risks that sunlight reflection could pose should be investigated, assessed, and weighed not in isolation, as if humans inhabited a perfect world, but alongside and against the *known* dangers, tensions, and inequities inherent in the experiment that humanity is currently, if unwittingly, running by pumping massive quantities of GHGs into the atmosphere. At present, the purported harms and benefits of SCI remain hypothetical, not demonstrated.[47] Indeed, some of the misgivings most frequently expressed concerning SCI are based on speculation rather than rigorous analysis and are thus more debatable than their proponents suggest.

The moral hazard and slippery slope objections to sunlight reflection and its research are influential claims in public discourse that rest on shaky ground. The former asserts that the prospect of SCI will inevitably displace mitigation efforts, giving humanity a so-called get-out-of-jail-free card to continue emitting GHGs. The latter contends that any research on the topic will invariably lead to SCI's deployment.[48] At first glance, both seem compelling. Given the possibility of a technological quick fix to the problem of global warming, why would countries assume the bother and expense of decarbonization? Wouldn't governments and citizens, egged on by fossil fuel companies, simply continue their polluting ways? Similarly, isn't it inevitable that setting up fully fledged national and international research programs on sunlight reflection will create incentives and dynamics to apply the resulting technology?

In fact, there is insufficient evidence to support either hypothesis.[49] As for the slippery slope argument, basic research and limited field experiments, if they reveal unacceptable and insurmountable risks, could well result in political authorities deciding *not* to attempt sunlight reflection. The field of pharmaceutical research, which often sees potential drugs abandoned if trials show them to be dangerous or ineffective, provides a useful analogy.[50] Moral hazard, meanwhile, is an ever-present feature of technological interventions, from seat belts to condoms and throughout the environmental realm.[51] Yet public opinion research provides scant empirical support for the proposition that the prospect of sunlight reflection displaces support for mitigation. The results vary depending on how the questions are framed.[52] Indeed, revealed preference surveys point to its inverse, suggesting that sunlight reflection could *increase* public support for emissions reductions by underscoring the gravity of the climate crisis.[53] The only way to find out is through more social science research.

Similar moral hazard arguments were once made with respect to both adaptation and CDR, both of which are broadly accepted today. The same could eventually be true of sunlight reflection. Policymakers should also consider the other side of the moral hazard argument: namely, if sunlight reflection is not adequately researched, future generations could be deprived of a potentially promising method to reduce excessive global heating.[54]

To understand the feasibility and effects of sunlight reflection, to weigh its risks relative to increased warming, and to make educated policy choices about its potential deployment, greater investments in both the physical and social sciences are needed.[55] All claims regarding the viability and consequences of SCI, positive or negative, need to be scrutinized rather than taken at face value.

THE NEED FOR A COMPARATIVE RISK ASSESSMENT

The potential risks and benefits of SCI, moreover, should be evaluated and weighed against Earth's current trajectory. As the IPCC's most recent assessment reports make clear, the long-awaited climate emergency is *now*.[56] Atmospheric CO_2 levels are the highest they have been in three million years—and the oceans more acidic than they have been in two million.[57] The past seven years have been the warmest on record.[58] Average global temperatures are on pace to rise 2.7 to 3°C (4.9 to 5.4°F) from preindustrial levels by 2100, and many of the resulting changes to Earth's natural systems will be "irreversible for centuries to millennia."[59]

For the past twelve thousand years, humanity has enjoyed marked climate stability, with average annual global temperatures rarely fluctuating more than 1°C (1.8°F). This benign era, which permitted the emergence of civilization, is over. The world is experiencing environmental changes the IPCC calls unprecedented in human history, among them the retreat of glaciers and Arctic sea ice, the breaking up of Antarctic ice shelves, dramatic warming and acidification of oceans, a poleward shift of Earth's climate zones, loss of species and ecosystems, and increased incidence of searing heat waves, punishing droughts, raging wildfires, heavy precipitation, and tropical cyclones. The coming decades will bring more of the same. How much more depends on how hot it gets. Because "every additional increment of global warming will dramatically increase the frequency of climatic and weather events," as the IPCC notes, a 1.5°C world is vastly preferable to a 2°C one. Even at 1.5°C, the repercussions will be severe.

More alarming still is the growing likelihood that a warming planet will experience abrupt, catastrophic shifts as Earth's natural systems cross critical thresholds, generating nonlinear changes that themselves accelerate climate change.[60] Such potential tipping points include a rapid dieback of the Amazon rainforest, a precipitous collapse of the Greenland and Antarctic ice sheets, an accelerated melting of permafrost that releases massive stores of methane and CO_2, and a swift shutdown of the Atlantic Meridional Overturning Circulation, an oceanic conveyor belt that helps keep northern Europe temperate and habitable.[61]

The costs of rising temperatures will be enormous, particularly for developing nations.[62] Global warming will hit the world's poorest communities hardest, endangering livelihoods, deepening poverty, and even rendering some regions uninhabitable. It will exacerbate water and food insecurity, create new vectors for infectious diseases, displace hundreds of millions of people, undermine the capacity and legitimacy of governments, and reinforce societal fissures, increasing the risks of violence in the world's forty-odd fragile states. Warming will also upend geopolitics, according to the National Intelligence Council (NIC), exacerbating diplomatic tensions and competition among the world's great powers.[63] In sum, the climate stage is already set for intensified international rivalry and instability.

For policymakers, the situation thus calls for a comparative risk assessment: Given the anticipated effects of climate change, are the risks to life on Earth likely to increase or decrease with the addition of sunlight reflection? To answer this question, officials need better knowledge of its feasibility and potential repercussions on both the natural and human worlds. This research agenda would ideally involve legal and ethical inquiry, including on the implications of sunlight reflection for equity, fairness, and justice.[64] Unfortunately, existing funding for such research is minuscule, a minute fraction of the hundreds of billions of dollars the world currently spends on mitigation and adaptation.[65]

U.S. ACTION ON SUNLIGHT REFLECTION TO DATE: ROOM FOR IMPROVEMENT

WHAT EXISTS NOW

Given the stakes, the U.S. government is, at present, severely under-investing in areas of science relevant to sunlight reflection and lacks a clear strategy to elevate and coordinate existing modest research efforts by U.S. agencies. The three main agencies with funded research in this field are the National Oceanic and Atmospheric Administration (NOAA), the Department of Energy (DOE), and the National Science Foundation (NSF). NOAA has a mandate to provide information on the state of the oceans and the atmosphere. Its small Earth's Radiation Budget program supports limited study on the climatic influence of aerosols from both anthropogenic and conventional sources, as well as measurements of the chemical composition of the atmosphere.[66] DOE is the primary locus for research on cloud-aerosol interactions in the troposphere, a lower layer of the atmosphere, and has impressive computing abilities for climate modeling. However, it has neither the funds nor the mandate to monitor the feasibility and effects of SAI or MCB. NSF, meanwhile, is the major funder of the National Center for Atmospheric Research and of university researchers working on climate science and climate change's wider societal, economic, environmental, and other effects. NSF also supports modeling studies from its engineering division.

Two other agencies merit mention. Although it does not support SCI research specifically, NASA has extensive programs in stratospheric and cloud-aerosol science and possesses aircraft and satellite platforms essential for observing the atmosphere. Finally, even though the Department of Defense (DOD) has been only a minor contributor to SCI-related science, the 2021 National Defense Authorization Act instructed the Office of Naval Research to review DOD and National Laboratories research needs for improving their understandings of aerosols' effects on clouds and sunlight reflection, in connection with DOD's operational and readiness requirements and the Pentagon's growing strategic concern with climate-related national security risks.[67]

Since 2018, Congress has quietly allocated, on a pragmatic, bipartisan basis, modest annual funding for NOAA and DOE to conduct atmospheric research focusing primarily on the stratosphere (relevant to SAI), but not for monitoring aerosol-cloud interactions in the troposphere (relevant to MCB). NOAA, for instance, has only $9 million in the current fiscal year for its Earth's Radiation Budget program, including the expenses associated with deploying instrumented weather balloons and renting specialized high-altitude aircraft (from NASA) to measure the state of the stratosphere. In late 2021, House and Senate appropriations committees approved some $11 million in fiscal year 2022 (FY 2022) federal funding to NOAA and between $15 million and $30 million to DOE for such research.[68] More generous support for both agencies is needed to provide a baseline understanding of the composition and dynamics of the upper and lower atmosphere, shed light on the feasibility of intentional climate interventions, and allow scientists to monitor any significant atmospheric shifts caused by climate change or by human intervention (whether publicly announced or clandestine). Those specific gaps in scientific knowledge cannot be filled by relying solely on NASA satellite data; routine sampling of the atmosphere is essential.[69]

The U.S. agencies currently conducting or supporting research relevant to sunlight reflection have done so with little White House guidance. Indeed, the Office of Science and Technology Policy (OSTP), which exists to coordinate investments in scientific research across the U.S. government, has been silent on the topic to date. The U.S. Global Change Research Program (USGCRP), an initiative involving thirteen U.S. agencies that operates under OSTP auspices, has also avoided any deliberations on sunlight reflection.[70] Seeking to stimulate executive branch action, Congress in March 2022 included three important provisions in the 2022 Consolidated Appropriations Act. It "encouraged" NOAA to develop, in coordination with OSTP and other agencies, an interagency program on "near-term climate hazard risk" management and intervention. It also directed NOAA to work with NASA and DOE to elucidate atmospheric aerosols' effects on the energy balance in the atmosphere. Finally, and most significantly, it ordered NOAA to "support" OSTP in the drafting of a report, due within 180 days of the legislation's enactment, on the research and development requirements for a subsequent, five-year assessment of potential "solar and other rapid climate interventions."[71] While these measures are good first steps, the legislation is vague on the contents of the envisioned NOAA report, the parameters of interagency assessment, and the respective coordinating roles of OSTP and USGCRP. Such a sustained vacuum of leadership risks undermining the strategic coherence and progress of U.S. efforts.

WHAT IS MISSING

The growing likelihood that Earth's average temperature will rise more than 2.5°C makes it imperative to improve policymakers' understanding of the immediate and near-immediate threats that such warming poses to human safety and well-being and of SCI's potential to offset these threats during the protracted transition to a carbon-neutral world. Significant lacunae in atmospheric and climate science, as well as uncertainties over the possible efficacy and repercussions of different SCI approaches, leave policymakers flying blind—ill-equipped to make educated and enlightened decisions about the application (or non-application) of such methods.

Filling those knowledge gaps will require the creation of a serious, well-funded, and effectively organized U.S. national research program, accompanied by a clear structure for research governance to ensure that such activities are conducted in a credible, safe, and responsible manner. Such an initiative could build on the findings of the landmark March 2021 report by the U.S. National Academies of Science, Engineering, and Medicine (NASEM), *Reflecting Sunlight: Recommendations for Solar Geoengineering Research and Governance*, and would equip policymakers in the United States and abroad with the information they need to make evidence-based decisions.[72]

An ideal governance framework would seek to distinguish between sunlight reflection research on the one hand and its prospective deployment on the other. To be sure, these undertakings can overlap. For instance, simple field experiments intended to shed light on the physics of SAI are clearly on the research side of the fence, whereas large-scale atmospheric experiments intended to illuminate the effects of SAI on global temperatures could shade into deployment. The vast majority of experiments currently contemplated, however, fall on the research side.

Any U.S. governance framework for sunlight reflection research would need to be tailored to the current moment, not least the increased politicization and suspicion surrounding scientific research. Winning public trust for a national SCI research program in the post-pandemic era would thus require an unequivocal commitment to transparency on the part of researchers and regulators, as well as sustained attention to combating misinformation. Even with such safeguards, a U.S. sunlight reflection research initiative is liable to be under attack from day one, making the question of risk assessment a divisive topic within and outside the scientific community, both domestically and internationally.

GAPS IN THE INTERNATIONAL GOVERNANCE OF SUNLIGHT REFLECTION

If the science of sunlight reflection remains in its infancy, its international governance has barely been conceived. Under current international law, national governments enjoy wide latitude to pursue SCI for peaceful purposes. No legally binding international instruments currently in force expressly regulate this activity. The law is not entirely silent, however. All nations have a due diligence obligation under customary international law to ensure that activities taken within sovereign borders do not generate significant transboundary environmental injuries (the so-called no harm rule). Some legal scholars argue that states also have a customary legal obligation to conduct environmental impact assessments of activities and notify and consult with potentially affected states.[73]

In addition, select multilateral treaties relevant to the environmental commons or specific environmental challenges establish important legal principles and set out germane state rights and responsibilities potentially relevant to sunlight reflection, depending on its effects. They include international conventions on climate change, transboundary air pollution, and biodiversity, among others (see box 1). Although none explicitly addresses sunlight reflection, these instruments collectively offer a basis to inform the negotiation of any future international legal regime to govern SCI. However, their direct applicability is limited. For example, while SCI undoubtedly constitutes "environmental modification," it would be exempted under the Convention on the Prohibition of Military or Any Other Hostile Use of Environmental Modification Techniques because SCI's implementation as a climate risk–management strategy would be for peaceful rather than hostile purposes.

Beyond the limited relevance of treaty law, the governance dilemmas posed by sunlight reflection are distinctive, restricting the direct applicability of international institutional design models from other transnational challenges or emerging technologies. The Nuclear Non-proliferation Treaty (NPT), which seeks to limit the spread of nuclear weapons while facilitating peaceful nuclear energy use, has been proposed as a possible model on which to build. The analogy, however, is fraught, both because the NPT's two-tier membership makes it a global hot-button issue and because the problem structure is different: the treaty is overwhelmingly about controlling dangerous weapons, whereas sunlight reflection is about discouraging unilateralism and promoting collaboration on a technology that carries risks but also potential rewards.[74]

Recent multilateral deliberations on gene drives—a gene-editing technology that results in living modified organisms—could perhaps offer a model for international research governance. Like sunlight reflection, this technology is inherently neither good nor evil—its moral measure depends on how it is studied and deployed. Facing calls to ban gene drives, the parties to the Convention on Biological Diversity in November 2018 agreed to certain limitations on their use. The experience suggests that it is possible not only to restrain the development of innovative technologies with potentially beneficial and negative applications rather than banning them outright, but also that such restraint can be achieved by balancing internationally negotiated ground rules with domestically retained control over case-specific project approval processes.[75]

At the diplomatic level, multilateral action on the governance of sunlight reflection has been negligible. In March 2019, for example, the consensus-based UN Environment Assembly (UNEA) failed to agree on a modest Swiss-led resolution, cosponsored by eleven diverse

Box 1. Multilateral Treaties of Relevance to Sunlight Reflection

UN Framework Convention on Climate Change

Sunlight reflection would not violate parties' obligations to stabilize emissions and could help achieve the Paris Agreement's temperature goals.

Vienna Convention for the Protection of the Ozone Layer and Its Montreal Protocol

Treaty would be relevant if sunlight reflection damaged the ozone layer.

Convention on Long-Range Transboundary Air Pollution (CLRTAP) and Its Protocols

Methods using sulfates could render parties noncompliant. Treaty applies only regionally in Europe.

UN Convention on the Law of the Sea (UNCLOS)

Treaty imposes a general commitment to environmental protection and no harm, but otherwise compatible with sunlight reflection.

London Convention and the Protocol on Prevention of Marine Pollution

Protocol is most relevant to marine geoengineering (e.g., fertilizing oceans to stimulate plankton growth) and has limited applicability to sunlight reflection.

Convention on Biological Diversity (CBD)

Nonbinding resolution discourages CBD parties from participating in "geoengineering" until there is adequate understanding of its potential effects.

Convention on International Civil Aviation

Materials most relevant to sunlight reflection are unlikely to be considered aircraft emissions, even if dispersed by aircraft.

Convention on the Prohibition of Military or Any Other Hostile Use of Environmental Modification Techniques (ENMOD)

Sunlight reflection exempted under "peaceful purposes" provisions.

Outer Space Treaty and Its Liability Convention

Treaty pertinent only in the case of space-based sunlight reflection efforts.

Human Rights (i.e., Universal Declaration; Covenants on Civil and Political and Economic, Social, and Cultural Rights; etc.)

Relevance would depend on sunlight reflection approaches, methods, and repercussions.

countries, calling on UNEP to "prepare an assessment of the status of geoengineering technologies" (including both sunlight reflection and CDR) and what if any governing frameworks would be applicable to them.[76] The United States, worried about heavy-handed international oversight of such research, led the effort to derail the resolution, arguing that scientific assessment should instead occur under IPCC auspices. Blame for the resolution's failure cannot be laid at U.S. feet alone, however. The episode exposed broader fissures among UNEA member states on whether such research should be endorsed and, if so, how stringently it should be governed.[77]

GOVERNING SUNLIGHT REFLECTION REQUIRES NAVIGATING ITS GEOPOLITICS

The current vacuum of international governance is worrisome because the relatively low cost of sunlight reflection could encourage unilateral action, posing what has been called a free-driver—as opposed to a free-rider—dilemma.[78] Whereas the main strategic challenge for emissions reductions is to *promote* collective action rather than shirking, the challenge in this case is to *discourage* countries from acting alone. As the pace of warming accelerates and its effects become more pronounced, a single nation-state (or a small group of countries) could be tempted to take matters into its (or their) own hands and launch a crash program of sunlight reflection. Other nations could well perceive such action as a potential threat to their vital interests, particularly if they anticipate that it will generate negative environmental, economic, or political externalities.

The NIC points to just this scenario in its landmark October 2021 *National Intelligence Estimate* (NIE). As international cooperation on climate change flounders, the NIC warns, governments of major powers could begin "unilaterally testing and deploying large scale solar geoengineering."[79] In the absence of shared scientific knowledge and in a climate of mistrust, such a provocative decision could be highly destabilizing. Indeed, the history of world politics teaches that uncertainty and anxiety can lead governments to make catastrophic miscalculations. Other countries would surely contest the right of any single nation or group of nations to set the world's thermostat, and they could well blame any natural disaster that happens to arise—whether related or unrelated—on these interventions. Governments could also threaten deployment as a form of environmental or technological blackmail, perhaps demanding greater action on climate mitigation and international adaptation financing in return for forgoing this option.[80]

It is easy to imagine sunlight reflection inflaming diplomatic tensions as governments disagree over whether and how to implement it; accuse others of deploying it surreptitiously; launch countermeasures or competing efforts of their own; denounce adversaries for inflicting harm, either inadvertently or with hostile intent; and demand compensation for perceived damages. While any unilateral steps to deploy sunlight reflection would presumably be motivated by a sense of acute environmental crisis, their practical effect would likely be to exacerbate the security dilemma inherent in world politics as other nations anticipate injuries to their vital interests. In an extreme case, governments could even seek to weaponize sunlight reflection to the disadvantage of their adversaries.[81] The mere suspicion of clandestine efforts to militarize SCI could stoke rivals' fears, prompting some to take ill-informed preventive action. In such a combustible context, resorting to violence cannot be ruled out.

Such prospective risks, however, should also be kept in perspective, because the geopolitical barriers to entry into this field—as opposed to the economic and technological ones—remain high.[82] In theory, scores of countries could obtain the financial resources and technical know-how to establish independent sunlight reflection programs in the near future—within, say, ten years.[83] They include most advanced market democracies, major emerging powers including the BRICS nations (Brazil, Russia, India, China, and South Africa), and even populous but poor developing countries confronting a daunting climate future, such as Bangladesh.

Introduce geopolitics, however, and the number of actors dwindles. Few national governments would presumably have the will or capability to act alone against a united multilateral system or, perhaps more to the point, to absorb the costs of defying or deterring retaliation from the world's great powers.[84] Given the possible censure, sanctions, or other punishments a freelancing country could face, the number of plausible candidates willing and able to deploy sunlight reflection unilaterally is likely to be no more than a dozen—a list that could include the United States, Brazil, China, France, Germany, India, Japan, Russia, the United Kingdom, the European Union (as a bloc), and perhaps a couple more. These same candidates, of course, also hold the answer to effective multilateral climate action generally, including within mini-lateral bodies such as the Group of Twenty (G20) and the Major Economics Forum (MEF).

The possibility of sunlight reflection could also scramble traditional geopolitical alignments. At first glance, one could expect leading

Western democracies to coordinate their positions on deployment. Success would hardly be assured, however. After all, the United States has often diverged markedly from its transatlantic allies over climate change policy (as well as other environmental issues, such as genetically modified organisms), and U.S. interest in sunlight reflection could reinforce allied mistrust over U.S. commitments to emissions abatement. Major European countries could also disagree among themselves over SCI's risks and benefits, just as France and Germany have adopted starkly different attitudes toward nuclear power. Given such national variations in risk tolerance and political culture, Western solidarity cannot be taken for granted.

In the current global context, the most volatile potential confrontation would presumably pit the United States against its leading authoritarian adversaries, China and Russia, particularly in the wake of the latter's February 2022 invasion of Ukraine. Once again, though, the geopolitics of sunlight reflection does not necessarily track with conventional strategic interests or ideological affinity. Notwithstanding the dangers posed by its fast-melting, methane-laden permafrost, Russia has to date adopted a more aloof stance toward climate change than China, which stands to suffer massively (and already has an advanced cloud-seeding program).[85] A shared concern on climate change could encourage China, which supported a modest national sunlight reflection research program between 2015 and 2019, to pursue scientific and technical cooperation on this issue with the United States, or even with its regional rival, India.[86] U.S.-China collaboration on the science of sunlight reflection and on the institutions needed for its governance would be a natural follow-up to the 2021 U.S.-China Joint Glasgow Declaration on Enhancing Climate Action in the 2020s.[87] Such technical cooperation could also help reduce bilateral tensions between the two countries. Beyond the great powers, the topic could either unify or divide major regional and subregional organizations such as the African Union, Association of Southeast Asian Nations, and Organization of American States, depending on whether their members agree or diverge in their estimations of its potential trade-offs.

In sum, the novel issue of sunlight reflection could upset longstanding partnerships—and create strange bedfellows. The fluid geopolitics of SCI and the intense controversy the topic elicits complicate global cooperation. A universal system of multilateral governance should remain the ultimate U.S. aspiration, but the United States should be prepared for the possibility that some states will participate only partially, or not at all, forcing it to explore novel configurations of cooperation. It should also be alert to the prospect that some countries may actively oppose work in this area, whether out of conviction, domestic political pressures, or strategic calculations.

This complex global context also complicates the already fraught question of U.S. leadership in the international governance of sunlight reflection. Until recently, the United States was accustomed to steering multilateral responses to many global challenges and having others defer to its direction. Those presumptions and expectations are less obvious and compelling today, thanks to the rise of competing power centers and world order visions, as well as lingering doubts abroad about U.S. credibility and staying power—not least on the topic of climate change. Concerted research efforts would more effectively advance mutual learning, whereas an overly assertive U.S. declaration of leadership to helm this global effort could be met with skepticism or hostility. The United States should thus aspire to partnership rather than leadership on SCI research. Such a cooperative stance could pay diplomatic dividends, reducing the prospects of disastrous decisions and geopolitical conflict.

PRIORITIES FOR COOPERATIVE INTERNATIONAL GOVERNANCE

Any international governance framework for sunlight reflection would ideally serve two broad purposes. First, it would provide national governments with access to consensus-based, high-quality, scientific assessments. Such data would ensure that policymakers worldwide have the same empirical basis on which to make informed decisions about the benefits and risks of using sunlight reflection— whether preventively, to ward off further warming, or reactively, as an emergency response to crossing a planetary tipping point. Second, it would provide governments with a high-level forum capable of making collective decisions on the basis of these assessments and other considerations about whether, how, and when to undertake such efforts, as well as of managing the risks of international conflict arising from disagreements. Those two roles, technical and political, are quite distinct, making it unlikely that a single institutional format would be able to discharge both effectively. No international framework currently performs either function.[88]

MULTILATERAL SCIENTIFIC ASSESSMENT

The first role of an international governance framework should be to provide UN member states with a common scientific understanding of the evolving risks posed by climate change and the potential for SCI techniques to ameliorate them. The 1988 Montreal Protocol on Substances that Deplete the Ozone Layer offers one promising model. Its three assessment panels provide treaty parties with authoritative, updated scientific knowledge on the status of the ozone layer, global effects of diminished ozone, and the development of innovative technologies to reduce its depletion. Those panels have helped make the

Montreal Protocol the most successful multilateral environmental treaty in history.[89]

A second example to emulate is the IPCC, which performs essentially the same assessment function but for the UNFCCC and which has become the world's premier independent source of climate science. With a track record spanning more than three decades, the IPCC enjoys widespread credibility, thanks to its reputation for providing governments with objective, comprehensive, and up-to-date scientific judgments while leaving policy prescriptions to others.

The world needs a similar intergovernmental assessment framework to ensure a shared, evolving scientific understanding of sunlight reflection's feasibility, risks, and benefits, both in general and in response to perceived climate tipping points. Such a common frame of reference is an essential precondition to negotiating global rules on SCI deployment. One tricky question is whether governments should seek to create a new multilateral assessment body or expand the mandate of an existing institution—potentially the IPCC itself. Both approaches have merit. A bespoke arrangement, analogous to the Intergovernmental Science-Policy Platform on Biodiversity and Ecosystem Services (IPBES), which has shed light on the dramatic degradation of Earth's natural capital, would have the benefits of a narrow focus, avoiding the risk that the issue of sunlight reflection becomes overwhelmed by other topics. On the other hand, embedding such discussions within the IPCC could help acclimatize governments to the idea of analyzing SCI as part of a broader portfolio of climate risk–management strategies, in the context of an anticipated climate overshoot.

To date, the IPCC has been reluctant to fully consider SCI, thanks to reticence among member states that designate its scientists. Its most recent assessment of the state of climate science in August 2021 included a cursory discussion of the potential effects of sunlight reflection, under various scenarios and on different components of the earth system, including the atmosphere, oceans, carbon and water cycles, and biodiversity. Tellingly, the IPCC excluded any mention of SCI from its top-line summary for policymakers, suggesting many governments still regard open discussion about it as controversial.[90]

HIGH-LEVEL COLLECTIVE DECISION-MAKING

In addition to this assessment function, the world needs another forum—or more likely forums—where governments can deliberate and take collective decisions about whether and how to deploy sunlight reflection techniques, as well as resolve disputes that arise among nations in this context.

To date, major international institutions have shied away from addressing the subject.[91] The failure of the 2019 UNEA resolution proposing a study of the topic is one case in point; that the issue has never even been discussed by UNFCCC parties is another. The hurdles to building consensus in such encompassing venues are admittedly high, given their susceptibility to regional political dynamics, ideological disagreements, and lowest-common-denominator outcomes. Such dynamics have been on full display at annual UNFCCC COPs, which have regularly pitted developed countries against developing ones on issues of historical responsibility, the burden of emissions reductions, and the magnitude of adaptation financing.

The prospect of sunlight reflection, however, could upend these traditional divisions by providing an avenue for strengthened North-South cooperation on climate change. Most developing countries are within vulnerable climate zones, lack adequate resources for adaptation, and will feel the brunt of global warming sooner and more sharply than developed countries will. As the costs of climate change become more obvious and acute, their governments could be drawn to SCI as a potential way to forestall an otherwise catastrophic rise in average global temperature, buying them time to survive the transition to a post-carbon world economy. This opens the possibility that SCI could be introduced, and eventually normalized, as a topic of deliberation at the annual UNFCCC COPs. Ensuring that developing nations are genuinely represented from the start in discussions about how to measure and define sunlight reflection's risks and rewards is therefore imperative.[92] Doing so could help blunt efforts by detractors and skeptics to frame SCI as a neo-imperialist plot imposed by the wealthy world; invigorate a much needed, indeed elemental, conversation about the comparative risks of sunlight reflection vis-à-vis unavoidable projected future warming; and enhance the equitable distribution of knowledge about SCI and promote its just governance.

Although universal agreement on the governance of sunlight reflection should remain an ultimate aspiration, the complexities of negotiations among 193 UN member states offer ample opportunities for recalcitrant countries and encrusted regional blocs to derail progress. To avoid holding the planet's fate hostage to such dynamics, and given the heterogeneity of global attitudes, the United States and other countries will likely need to adopt a heterodox approach to the multilateral governance of SCI, relying simultaneously and for different purposes on universal forums that bring the benefits of inclusivity, great power arrangements that carry the advantages of effectiveness, and partnerships of like-minded nations that promise the rewards of solidarity.[93] Two recurrent challenges will be finding the right balance between relying on encompassing bodies versus more exclusive frameworks and ensuring complementarity and connection among these formats.

Finally, it is imperative that any institution-building effort designed to govern the research, development, and deployment of sunlight reflection should complement and reinforce—rather than compete with and undermine—emissions cuts, CDR, and adaptation. Managing the interaction and ensuring the complementarity among these four lines of effort will be a critical benchmark of success.

RECOMMENDATIONS

For too long, the topic of sunlight reflection has been a third rail of climate change discourse, limiting both basic research and diplomatic discussion. That situation is starting to change as the devastating implications of a fast-warming planet become impossible to ignore. Given the escalating threat to both social and natural systems posed by rising temperatures, the world needs to improve its collective understanding of the feasibility and risks of this option, as well as strive for international agreement on the norms and rules that should govern its potential (non)application.

To help further those objectives, the United States should take the following steps:

ON A DOMESTIC LEVEL

Develop a Robust U.S. Sunlight Reflection Research Program

The Joe Biden administration should use its existing authorities to launch a robust, cooperative, and transdisciplinary government-wide research program on sunlight reflection, grounded in international cooperation, as recommended by NASEM's March 2021 report. Its purpose should be to better understand the feasibility, benefits, risks, and effects of SCI and support evidence-based decision-making about whether to include it in humanity's portfolio of climate risk–management strategies.[94] It would thus greatly expand the narrower interagency effort envisioned in the 2022 omnibus appropriations package.[95]

Such a U.S. research program should seek to provide an analytical foundation for weighing the relative risks of climate change with and without sunlight reflection efforts in the following ways:

- deepen U.S. and global understanding of evolving climate threats, including the proximity of natural-system tipping points and their potential consequences, as a basis for further investigation—unfortunately this sort of analysis is not yet being done systematically within the U.S. government;

- assess whether sunlight reflection methods could reduce these risks;

- evaluate the possible dangers such interventions could pose for the environment, the economy, society, and global security;

- incorporate knowledge and perspectives from a wide array of natural and social sciences, including climatology, meteorology, chemistry, physics, engineering, political science, economics, ethics and philosophy, and law;

- clarify the technological and other requirements to launch and bring any climate interventions to scale;

- analyze the global political implications of alternative approaches to sunlight reflection research and implementation, with the State Department and intelligence community taking the lead on these efforts; and

- define the institutional requirements for effective national and global governance of sunlight reflection research and any potential deployment.[96]

This national research effort should be guided by the following principles:

- facilitate an evidence-based approach to decision-making, in which neither the use nor prohibition of sunlight reflection is predetermined;

- adopt a symmetrical approach to precaution, weighing the risks and uncertainties of sunlight reflection in the broader context of climate change;

- ensure transparency through information sharing and by facilitating scrutiny from policymakers and the public; and

- place international scientific collaboration among diverse governments and researchers at the forefront of this program.[97]

Capitalizing on existing authorities and the nascent efforts introduced in the 2022 omnibus bill, the Biden administration should assign the Office of Science and Technology Policy responsibility for coordinating this national research program, drawing on and augmenting the unique capabilities of relevant U.S. agencies, including those already participating in SCI-applicable science. OSTP should direct the U.S. Global Change Research Program to launch an interagency study of research priorities across the federal government, with an eye to promoting an effective division of labor, as well as informing decisionmakers and the public about the relative risks and repercussions of sunlight reflection versus warming.

The White House should also explicitly commit the United States to a collaborative approach toward both research and future deployment decisions. Doing so would help alleviate global mistrust about U.S. intentions and concerns about secret national programs worldwide. An alternative U.S. strategy of pursuing a classified, unilateral research program would likely backfire, contributing to mutual suspicion and rivalry, encouraging reciprocal action, and undermining cooperation to reduce climate risk.

Hold Congressional Hearings on U.S. Responses to Climate Risk

In parallel with these executive branch efforts, the Congressional Select Committee on the Climate Crisis, which includes both Senate and House members, should launch hearings on managing climate risk. Those hearings should:

- assess the projected immediate and near-immediate dangers to human safety and well-being, as well as other U.S. national interests, posed by accelerating climate change;

- evaluate the prospects of successfully addressing those threats through emissions reductions, CDR, and adaptation; and

- consider what potential additions to this portfolio of strategies, including SCI, could become warranted if the world confronts a dramatic temperature overshoot.

To be sure, such hearings could be risky in today's highly charged political and media environment. The topic of sunlight reflection research could well become partisan, with critics accusing supporters of shilling for fossil fuel industries and supporters blasting opponents for ignoring a fast-acting, cost-effective innovation with the potential to reduce human suffering.

Pass Enabling Legislation

Congress should formally establish the aforementioned U.S. research program through legislation specifying its mandate, objectives, timelines, institutional structure, regulatory requirements, and funding mechanisms. The legislation should be informed by the assessment provided to OSTP based on the 2022 omnibus appropriations package. The legislation should:

- direct the White House to provide Congress with regular scientific and assessment reports on immediate or anticipated climate risks, as well as on the evolving state of climate intervention methodologies and their potential effects;

- establish federal oversight of SCI experiments, whether undertaken by public or private entities, conducted within the territory of the United States or by its citizens in areas beyond national jurisdiction (including the high seas, Antarctica, the atmosphere, or outer space); and

- help close regulatory gaps in existing U.S. statutes, including the Weather Modification Act, Clean Air Act, Endangered Species Act, and National Environmental Policy Act, which all establish important legal principles and processes (e.g., the need for environmental impact assessments) but do not explicitly address sunlight reflection.

Secure and Provide Adequate Funding and Authorities

The White House should request, and Congress approve, a major expansion of the authorities and budgets of NOAA, DOE, NSF, the State Department, and—more narrowly—DOD. This legislative action should include the following specific measures:

- Pass an updated version of the Atmospheric Climate Intervention Research Act (H.R. 5519) to expand NOAA's authorities and capabilities to measure, monitor, and report on the composition, chemistry, and dynamics of atmospheric gases and aerosols; establish and rapidly expand NOAA's capabilities and platforms to better observe the atmosphere from the ocean, troposphere, and stratosphere; and broaden the agency's Earth's Radiation Budget program to increase investment in relevant atmospheric science and encompass research on SCI's potential to mitigate climate risks, building on Congress' directives in the 2022 omnibus bill.[98]

- Expand the authorities and capabilities of DOE and its labs to research cloud-aerosol interactions in the lower atmosphere, including through enhanced observational studies, modeling, computing, and small-scale experiments. A better understanding of the sensitivity of clouds to aerosols (ranging from salt crystals to black carbon) and their interactions is critical to better understanding weather patterns, analyzing climate risks, and gauging the viability of MCB as a counterstrategy to the warming effect of GHGs. The expansion of DOE cloud aerosol research called for in the 2022 omnibus bill is a start; however, clearly defined and broader authorities are needed to address the range of concerns and possible implications associated with SCI experimentation and deployment.

- Direct NSF to channel increased funding to sunlight reflection-relevant research. This funding should include support for studies on approaching climate tipping points and the potential for SCI methods to help forestall them. NSF grants should also support policy-relevant social science research that could illuminate the trade-offs, risks, and uncertainties of sunlight reflection, including its implications for social welfare, peace, and justice; shed light on the political economy of deployment decisions, including the role of incentives, norms, and institutions in fostering international cooperation; and suggest how the world could optimize its mix of climate risk–management strategies.[99]

- Empower the State Department to lead U.S. diplomatic efforts to advance international cooperation on sunlight reflection, including science and technology cooperation and the negotiation of international norms and rules to govern any future implementation decisions. The Bureau of Oceans and International Environmental and Scientific Affairs should lead and coordinate this U.S. diplomatic push.

- Narrowly expand DOD's authorities and resources to conduct sunlight reflection research relevant to its mandate. This is a delicate matter, given the importance of international collaboration and the risks of appearing to militarize sunlight reflection by granting a role to the Pentagon. Congress should therefore focus any expanded DOD authorities and funding on improving the United States' ability to monitor other countries' deployment of such technologies—a legitimate, defensive purpose. Improving such capabilities would also provide a degree of mutual international reassurance against unilateral action by increasing the likelihood that any clandestine efforts would be detected.

Total annual budgetary outlays for this effort should begin at $300 million and increase by approximately $50 million per year to reach $500 million by year five. This budget should support research on atmospheric processes related to sunlight reflection, particularly climate-aerosol interactions; sunlight reflection's effects on the climate and other natural systems; its political, economic, and ethical implications; the prerequisites for its effective national and international governance; and the technological and engineering requirements of any eventual deployment.

Addressing the immediate need for more research and knowledge, this proposed budget represents a massive expansion in current agency outlays and a more than ten-fold increase in the amount envisioned in the 2021 NASEM report, which called for $100 million to $200 million in total federal support for sunlight reflection research over five years. This enlargement, however, is phased in and capped to account for agencies' capacities to absorb funding.[100] Furthermore, while this allocation could seem like a radical increase from the NASEM recommendation, it pales in comparison to the $4.82 billion in total spending for USGCRP climate-related research activities by U.S. federal agencies in the Biden administration's FY 2022 budget.[101] It is also modest relative to its FY 2022 budget for research and development within DOE itself, which includes more than $1.85 billion for nuclear energy research; $890 million for "fossil energy and carbon management" research; and $700 million for energy and climate research by the department's Advanced Research Project Agency. Congress appropriated more than $7 billion for DOE's Office of Science alone in FY 2021.[102] More generally, the proposed $300 million in federal spending in year one is less than one-quarter of 1 percent of the $150 billion in climate-related spending included in the recent infrastructure bill, and less than 1/2,500th (0.04 percent) of the $750 billion the DOD receives to counter more traditional security threats.[103] Finally, the size of this outlay also addresses the minimal role the private sector will likely play in sunlight reflection research and development, in contrast to CDR, given the relatively low scale of required investment and the inherently limited market for SCI-related technology and equipment beyond modest public procurement.[104]

Adopt a Balanced Approach to SCI Research Governance

To build public trust in this controversial field and safeguard against potential risks, the United States should adopt a serious but balanced approach to the governance of sunlight reflection research. The goal should be to introduce some basic ground rules without hindering essential scientific inquiry that could help the world stave off catastrophic warming. This governance framework should distinguish between modest projects that present minimal dangers and large-scale research activities that begin to cross the line into deployment, with unforeseen consequences. Regulators, which should be identified from within existing competent U.S. agencies, should avoid imposing too great a precautionary burden on activities that pose infinitesimal risks lest they strangle essential research in the crib.[105] The wisest course would be to adjust protocols and rules to the scope and scale of research ambitions so that the stringency of oversight and the hurdles for approval grow as researchers move from modeling, to laboratory work, to field experiments.[106]

Drawing on input from its member agencies, the USGCRP should classify field experiments into three tiers, based on scientific thresholds, with governance requirements increasing with their scale, intensity, and significance. Those conducted on a small scale and posing insignificant risks would require no additional regulation besides registration and an environmental impact assessment; those conducted on a medium to large scale and posing potential hazards would require a more detailed environmental impact statement and rigorous approval process; and those with the possibility of significant transboundary impacts would not be allowed at this time.[107] Additionally, any research projects involving the deliberate release of sunlight-reflecting substances into the atmosphere should be undertaken only when they can accelerate understanding or provide knowledge not available through laboratory studies or computer modeling.

To promote societal trust and counter misinformation, the U.S. government should promote transparency and data sharing among researchers and maintain a regularly updated, publicly available national registry of any field experiments undertaken by the U.S. government or private actors. The registry would include advance notice of plans and objectives and complete and timely disclosure of results.[108] There is, of course, no guarantee that public controversy will not erupt. However, it is possible to mitigate that risk through transparency, data sharing, and public disclosure.

Critics of SCI research often lobby for onerous and protracted public consultation and consent processes, sometimes in hope of throwing sand in the gears, but the appropriate primary locus for ensuring democratic accountability and oversight should remain the people's elected congressional representatives. The regulatory process for sunlight reflection research should therefore provide opportunities for public notice and comment, but not public veto. Relevant analogies are the processes for government authorization of new agricultural chemicals, approval of vaccines and medical devices, or standard setting for vehicle emissions. These afford agencies significant leeway to make decisions within regulatory guidelines, subject to congressional oversight.

Finally, rather than creating entirely new mechanisms to review, approve, and supervise field research projects, the United States should, where possible, rely on existing government agencies and institutions (e.g., NOAA and DOE) that currently possess a mandate to oversee publicly funded research and relevant laws. Atmospheric tests, for instance, would fit within the definition of "weather modification" under the Weather Modification Reporting Act, which provides an adequate framework for reporting and transparency on sunlight reflection experiments.[109]

Analyze and Manage the Geopolitics of Sunlight Reflection Vis-à-vis U.S. and International Interests

President Biden should commission an NIE on sunlight reflection geopolitics to improve the United States' (and the world's) understanding of the evolving international security landscape. Based on this study, the White House should conduct interagency exercises and/or tabletop simulations playing out possible scenarios, including multilateral crisis response options, should another government pursue unilateral deployment. U.S. officials should be mindful that national attitudes on sunlight reflection could diverge from traditional geopolitical alignments, opening the possibility for cooperative approaches with strategic rivals, including China.

ON AN INTERNATIONAL LEVEL

Reassure Others About U.S. Intentions

To avoid signaling to foreign actors that any type of behavior is allowed and to allay concerns about U.S. intentions, the U.S. government should declare that it will undertake the following steps:

- refrain from authorizing any major sunlight reflection interventions, including field research experiments by U.S. agencies or private actors, independently or without notice, above a specified threshold;

- disavow any intention to deploy SCI technologies unilaterally and seek to immediately begin conversations on sunlight reflection research with China and other major powers;

- notify any potentially affected states prior to any experiments that could have significant transboundary effects; and

- support a temporary global moratorium (as opposed to a permanent, unconditional ban) on interventions, including experiments, that could have material effects on the world's climate.[110]

Support International Research Collaboration

In addition to making multilateral scientific collaboration a cornerstone of its national research program, the United States should enlist all interested nations, including erstwhile strategic competitors, in a common scientific enterprise, promote adherence to shared norms and research codes of conduct, and encourage common frameworks and standards for assessing empirical evidence.[111] To manifest these principles and objectives, the United States should:

- create a global digital clearinghouse where governments and scientists can collect and share data on research and experiments, gain access to models and tools, and scrutinize projects to ensure they meet precautionary and legal standards and encourage public disclosure;

- leverage existing platforms for scientific cooperation such as the Inter-Academy Council, the International Science Council, the World

Climate Research Program, and the Inter-American Institute for Global Change Research; and

- routinely share information about U.S.-based projects and findings with the IPCC, UNEP, the World Meteorological Organization (WMO), and the Montreal Protocol Assessment Panel, encouraging other governments to do likewise.[112]

At a more ambitious level, the United States and its international partners should consider the track record of scientific mega-projects, such as the European Organization for Nuclear Research (CERN) and the International Space Station (ISS), as potential models for sustained research collaboration on sunlight reflection.[113] While such joint research need not occur at a single physical location, the United States should explore mechanisms to encourage similar cooperative projects, including the pooling of national funds to support multinational scientific teams.

Recognizing SCI's potential for improving North-South cooperation on climate matters and the importance of elevating the perspectives of developing nations, the United States should, from the outset, treat developing countries, including those most vulnerable to climate change, as full partners in any multilateral sunlight reflection research efforts. This includes research into SCI's feasibility, risks, costs, and benefits (including defining the metrics informing this calculus). Such collaboration currently occurs only through nongovernmental channels, most notably the Degrees (formerly the Solar Radiation Management Governance) Initiative, which links scientists in several developing nations with European and North American counterparts.[114] Given its unparalleled scientific expertise, the United States is likely to find its own well-designed, responsible research program becoming a model for other nations to emulate—a common historical pattern in the diffusion of scientific research and environmental policy.[115]

At the same time, given the uneven U.S. record on climate policy and the desire to alleviate potential suspicions of its intentions, the United States should focus on nurturing effective partnerships rather than proclaiming U.S. global leadership in research. Such an approach would not only build scientific capacity in partner nations but also promote global trust and legitimacy and more effectively advance mutual learning on the potential local and regional consequences of solar climate interventions.[116]

Promote the IPCC as the Authoritative Body for Regular
Scientific Assessments

The United States should enlist other governments to make sunlight reflection a core focus of the IPCC's seventh assessment report (AR7), due out in several years' time. More immediately, the United States should push for an IPCC interim special report assessing the scientific and technical feasibility of sunlight reflection and its potential repercussions as a response to climate overshoot. This initiative, akin to the panel's influential 2018 *Special Report on Global Warming of 1.5°C*, should include several specialized workshops under IPCC auspices and, if possible given existing knowledge and capacities, inform policymakers about the varying degrees of potential consequences (e.g., local, national, regional, or global) associated with different types of SCI experimentation.[117] The IPCC should also collaborate with other international bodies, such as the UNEP, WMO, IPBES, and the International Energy Agency, in assessing the potential role of sunlight reflection as part of the Paris Agreement's planned 2023 "global stocktake."[118]

Activate a Broad Array of Multilateral Forums

Recognizing the benefits of cultivating the broadest possible international buy-in, and encouraging North-South convergence, the United States should support expanded discussions on sunlight reflection within universal-membership bodies such as the UN General Assembly (UNGA) and the UNEA, as well as greater attention to SCI among parties to the UNFCCC negotiating process, including at the upcoming COP27 in Sharm el-Sheikh, Egypt. Integrating SCI into the COP process in particular will help normalize it as a potential climate risk–management strategy that warrants serious consideration by international policymakers. The United States should encourage responsible developing country governments to actively lead these deliberations. It should also urge the governments of Kenya and Sweden to put the issue on the agenda of the UN high-level meeting they will jointly host in June 2022 to commemorate the fiftieth anniversary of the 1972 United Nations Conference on the Human Environment (or Stockholm Conference).

As part of this effort, the United States should call on the UN secretary-general to appoint an independent, high-level global commission on the risks of sunlight reflection, with a political mandate to propose how the world should govern its large-scale research and potential deployment.[119] These proposals, which should include provisions for transparency, monitoring, attribution, and dispute resolution, could be presented to UNGA or the UNEA and help inform an eventual international convention. Despite their mixed historical performance, high-level commissions have at times helped define basic principles and drive policy initiatives on topics as diverse as sustainable development (e.g., the Brundtland Commission) and mass atrocities (e.g., International Commission on Intervention and State Sovereignty).[120]

While universal agreement on sunlight reflection should remain the ultimate U.S. objective, the United States should also use its permanent UN Security Council seat to focus that more selective body on the need to manage the growing geopolitical and security risks of climate overshoot, including through international collaboration on sunlight reflection research and governance. Although the UN Security Council has historically resisted addressing the linkages between climate change and security (most recently in December 2021), that posture will likely become untenable as the gravity of the global environmental emergency deepens and the prospect of unilateral SCI deployment—which arguably has more overt implications for international security than climate change alone—grows.[121] Introducing the topic in the UN Security Council, beginning in May 2022 when it holds the rotating presidency, would signal the United States' desire to neutralize potential conflict over SCI and forge a common approach to its governance with fellow permanent members China and Russia, notwithstanding obvious and ongoing geopolitical tensions with both nations, particularly in the aftermath of Russia's invasion of Ukraine.

Simultaneously, the United States should add SCI to the summit agendas and ministerial activities of the G20 and the climate-focused MEF. Although neither grouping is capable of taking binding decisions, these two consultative venues offer useful settings for the United States to try to build bridges and harmonize approaches on sunlight reflection with important parties, including significant emerging economies such as Brazil, India, Indonesia, Saudi Arabia, South Africa, and Turkey. An alternative would be to create a stand-alone mini-lateral mechanism for this purpose, but it could be redundant given that its membership would likely parallel that of the G20 and MEF.

Finally, the United States should encourage intensive SCI research collaboration and seek agreement within the more exclusive club of developed democratic partners on the principles, norms, and rules required to govern SCI's deployment, with the ultimate purpose of driving broader global cooperation. To accomplish this, Washington should push to make sunlight reflection a standing agenda item in annual Group of Seven (G7), North Atlantic Treaty Organization (NATO), and U.S.-EU summits and encourage new, year-round deliberations and analyses on the topic involving the ministries of relevant governments. The United States should also integrate discussions of sunlight reflection in its bilateral diplomacy with other advanced market democracies and allies, including Australia and South Korea.

While there is no guarantee that (generally) like-minded governments will reach common ground on this tricky issue, their common support for democratic values and the rule of law, as well as their shared economic and geopolitical interests, are likely to narrow the range of or at least cushion the fallout from potential policy divergence. That has been the case with genetically modified organisms, for instance, in which the U.S. and European partners have sought and attempted peaceful resolution of disputes (including through World Trade Organization arbitration). Seeking solidarity among fellow advanced market democracies should thus remain a priority for U.S. policymakers and diplomats. The success of this diplomacy will hinge in part on persuading allies that U.S. support for research on and the governance of sunlight reflection will reinforce rather than displace U.S. commitments to emissions abatement.

Discourage a Restrictive International Treaty on SCI Research Governance, for Now

At this stage, a binding international treaty to govern sunlight reflection research, specifying what should be permitted and under what auspices, is not needed. Efforts to negotiate such a formal agreement would be time consuming and possibly futile at a moment when the world finds itself at a perilous juncture of the future of Earth's climate and desperately in need of basic scientific insights about the feasibility of sunlight reflection and the risks, costs, and rewards of alternative approaches. Such negotiations could well result in misguided or ill-informed regulations, leading to shortsighted restrictions or even outright prohibitions on fundamental research before scientists have generated the knowledge policymakers need to identify and weigh relevant considerations.

Design Multilateral Governance Frameworks That Complement and
Reinforce Other Climate Risk–Management Strategies

Lastly, to reduce the risk of moral hazard, the United States should seek to enhance linkages between sunlight reflection and emissions abatement. One promising approach would be to make participation in a multilateral body created to govern SCI—particularly one responsible for future deployment decisions—conditional on a nation's commitment to and realization of emissions reductions. The success of such linkage would of course depend on how strongly any particular government desires a seat at the governing table and on whether it considers the threat of exclusion credible.[122] It also assumes that the United States, despite intense internal political divisions, will redouble its domestic commitments to mitigation, rather than using the prospect of sunlight reflection as an excuse to delay decarbonization.

CONCLUSION

The long-predicted climate emergency is now. As global temperatures climb, so do the stakes of living in a changing climate on a planet knocked out of balance. The approaches currently being pursued to prevent catastrophic warming and mute its implications are not being enacted fast enough. Considering the risks climate change poses to human safety and well-being, it is untenable for governments to ignore any potential supplementary approach that could limit the dangers posed by disastrous temperature increases. Sunlight reflection is such a potential stopgap strategy that could—in light of current warming trends and risk projections—make what is likely to be a lengthy transition to a decarbonized world tolerable. It is thus incumbent on countries to assess the feasibility and wisdom of pursuing this option and the institutions required to govern its potential deployment.

As the climate emergency deepens, governments facing mounting challenges to their national security, prosperity, health, development, and, in certain latitudes, even basic survival could decide to pursue unilateral climate intervention measures. In the absence of shared knowledge and rules, they would be acting with limited to no understanding of the consequences, amidst heightened geopolitical tensions, and in a vacuum of international norms and accountability structures. It would be vastly preferable for the world to make progress on the science of sunlight reflection and to discuss its national and international governance openly today, so that policymakers are prepared to make informed decisions on its potential deployment tomorrow, rather than being forced to act out of ignorance on the fly when all other options have failed.[123]

The current, perilous moment calls for extensive international research collaboration and negotiation of global ground rules for the possible use of SCI as a complement to GHG emissions reductions, CDR, and adaptation. The United States, which has an unsurpassed track record of scientific and technological innovation and an admirable legacy of inspiring new multilateral institutions, should be at the heart of this global effort.

ENDNOTES

1. Other common terms include solar radiation modification and albedo modification.

2. For a good survey of the ethics of sunlight reflection, see Stephen M. Gardiner, Catriona McKinnon, and Augustin Fragnière, ed., *The Ethics of "Geoengineering" the Climate: Governance, Legitimacy and Justice* (Milton Park, UK: Routledge, 2020).

3. See Sikina Jinnah and Simon Nicholson, "The Hidden Politics of Climate Engineering," *Nature Geoscience* 12 (October 2019): 876–79, https://www.nature.com/articles/s41561-019-0483-7.

4. See Jesse L. Reynolds, *The Governance of Solar Geoengineering* (Cambridge, UK: Cambridge University Press, 2019).

5. See SilverLining, "Near-Term Imperatives for Comprehensive Climate Policy: Silver-Lining Recommendations for the Biden-Harris Administration Plan for Climate Change and Environmental Justice" (Washington, DC: SilverLining, 2021), https://static1.squarespace.com/static/5bbac81c7788975063632c65/t/5fe0cf832402285551ec984c/1608568707219/SL+Report+Near-Term+Imperatives.pdf.

6. See "What Are Nature-Based Solutions?," Fact Sheet: Nature-Based Solutions to Climate Change, American University's School of International Service, accessed January 12, 2022, https://www.american.edu/sis/centers/carbon-removal/fact-sheet-nature-based-solutions-to-climate-change.cfm; and National Academies of Sciences, Engineering, and Medicine, *Negative Emissions Technologies and Reliable Sequestration: A Research Agenda* (Washington, DC: National Academies Press, 2019), https://doi.org/10.17226/25259.

7. See Brad Plummer and Raymond Zhong, "Climate Change Is Harming the Planet Faster Than We Can Adapt, UN Warns," *New York Times*, February 28, 2022, https://www.nytimes.com/2022/02/28/climate/climate-change-ipcc-report.html; and Richard J.T. Klein et al., "Chapter 16: Adaptation, Opportunities, Constraints and Limits," in *Special Report: Global Warming of 1.5°C* (Geneva: Intergovernmental Panel on Climate Change, 2018): 899–943, https://www.ipcc.ch/site/assets/uploads/2018/02/WGIIAR5-Chap16_FINAL.pdf.

8. The IPCC's latest assessment reports reveal that nations are not doing nearly enough to reduce greenhouse gas emissions or remove atmospheric CO_2 and that radical

climate action is needed to preserve a stable and hospitable planet for humanity. See Intergovernmental Panel on Climate Change Working Group II, *Climate Change 2022: Impacts, Adaptation, and Vulnerability* (Geneva: Intergovernmental Panel on Climate Change, 2022), https://report.ipcc.ch/ar6wg2/pdf/IPCC_AR6_WGII_FinalDraft _FullReport.pdf; and Intergovernmental Panel on Climate Change Working Group III, *Climate Change 2022: Mitigation of Climate Change* (Geneva: Intergovernmental Panel on Climate Change, 2022), https://report.ipcc.ch/ar6wg3/pdf/IPCC_AR6_WGIII _FinalDraft_FullReport.pdf.

9. See Robert "Bobby" Whitescarver, "Atmospheric Carbon Dioxide Highest in 3 Million Years: Column," *Newsleader*, June 22, 2021, https://www.newsleader.com/story/opinion /columnists/2021/06/22/atmospheric-co-2-carbon-dioxide-concentration-rising /5307791001; for figure 1 source of data, see "Trends in Atmospheric Carbon Dioxide," Global Monitoring Laboratory, accessed February 3, 2022, https://gml.noaa.gov/ccgg /trends/mlo.html.

10. See "Global Climate Change Explorer," Exploratorium, accessed January 12, 2022, https://www.exploratorium.edu/climate/atmosphere.

11. See UN Environment Program and UN Environment Program DTU Partnership, *Emissions Gap Report* 2021 (Nairobi: UN Environment Program, 2021), https://www .unep.org/resources/emissions-gap-report-2021.

12. Accounting for the realization of updated nationally determined contributions, global emissions (excluding land use) are set to rise by 16.3 percent from 2010 levels. See UN Framework Convention on Climate Change, *Nationally Determined Contributions Under the Paris Agreement: Synthesis Report by the Secretariat*, FCCC/PA/CMA/2021/8 (Bonn: UN Framework Convention on Climate Change, 2021), 5, https://unfccc.int /sites/default/files/resource/cma2021_08_adv_1.pdf.

13. See Fatih Birol, "COP26 Climate Pledges Could Help Limit Global Warming to 1.8°C, but Implementing Them Will Be the Key," International Energy Agency, November 2, 2021, https://www.iea.org/commentaries/cop26-climate-pledges-could-help-limit-global -warming-to-1-8-c-but-implementing-them-will-be-the-key.

14. See UN Environment Program and UN Environment Program DTU Partnership, "Addendum to the Emissions Gap Report 2021" (Nairobi: UN Environment Program, 2021), https://wedocs.unep.org/bitstream/handle/20.500.11822/37350/AddEGR21 .pdf; and Zeke Hausfather and Piers Forster, "Analysis: Do COP26 Promises Keep Global Warming Below 2C?," Carbon Brief, November 11, 2021, https://www.carbonbrief .org/analysis-do-cop26-promises-keep-global-warming-below-2c; for figure 2 source of data, see "Temperatures," Climate Action Tracker, accessed February 3, 2022, https:// climateactiontracker.org/global/temperatures.

15. See National Academies of Sciences, Engineering, and Medicine, *A Research Strategy for Ocean-Based Carbon Dioxide Removal and Sequestration* (Washington, DC: National Academies Press, 2021), https://doi.org/10.17226/26278.

16. See Ben Panko, "World's Largest Carbon Capture Plant Opens in Iceland," *Smithsonian Magazine*, September 9, 2021, https://www.smithsonianmag.com/smart-news/worlds -largest-carbon-capture-plant-opens-iceland-180978620.

17. This comparison is based on comments made by novelist Neal Stephenson at a book presentation and verified by independent calculations based on the mass of carbon in

anthropogenically emitted CO_2 (3.13 x 10^{14} kilograms), the density of pure graphite (0.002 kilograms per centimeter cubed), the volume of anthropogenic carbon dioxide as pure graphite (37.54 miles cubed), the density of rock (2.7 grams per centimeter cubed), the volume of Mount Rainier (90 miles cubed), and the mass of Mount Rainier based on its volume (1.01 x 10^{16} kilograms). Exact calculations can be made available upon request. The author is grateful to Dr. Sarah Doherty for her assistance in verifying this comparison. See also Neal Stephenson, "Termination Shock" (presentation, Long Now Foundation Long Now Talks, San Francisco, November 17, 2021).

18. The IPCC's most recent assessment report on the implications of climate change summarizes the current shortcomings and inherent limits of adaptation efforts. See Intergovernmental Panel on Climate Change Working Group II, *Climate Change 2022: Impacts, Adaptation, and Vulnerability*; and "Step Up Climate Change Adaptation or Face Serious Human and Economic Damage: UN Report," UN Environmental Programme, January 14, 2021, https://www.unep.org/news-and-stories/press-release /step-climate-change-adaptation-or-face-serious-human-and-economic.

19. See Paul Crutzen, "Albedo Enhancement by Stratospheric Sulfur Injections: A Contribution to Resolve a Policy Dilemma?," *Climatic Change* 77 (July 2006): 211–19, https:// doi.org/10.1007/s10584-006-9101-y.

20. See Peter J. Irvine and David W. Keith, "Halving Warming With Stratospheric Aerosol Geoengineering Moderates Policy-Relevant Climate Hazards," *Environmental Research Letters* 15, no. 044011 (2020), https://iopscience.iop.org/article/10.1088/1748-9326 /ab76de/pdf; Graham Readfearn, "Scientists Trial Cloud Brightening Equipment to Shade and Cool Great Barrier Reef," *Guardian*, April 16, 2020, https://www.theguardian .com/environment/2020/apr/17/scientists-trial-cloud-brightening-equipment-to-shade -and-cool-great-barrier-reef; and National Academies of Sciences, Engineering, and Medicine, *Climate Intervention: Reflecting Sunlight to Cool Earth* (Washington, DC: National Academies Press, 2015), https://doi.org/10.17226/18988.

21. See Gernot Wagner, *Geoengineering: The Gamble* (Cambridge, UK: Polity Press, 2021), 20; and Alan Robock, "Benefits and Risks of Stratospheric Solar Radiation Management for Climate Intervention (Geoengineering)," *The Bridge*, 50 (Spring 2020): 59–67, http://climate.envsci.rutgers.edu/pdf/RobockBridge.pdf.

22. See Intergovernmental Panel on Climate Change, *Special Report: Global Warming of 1.5°C* (Geneva: Intergovernmental Panel on Climate Change, 2018), https://www.ipcc .ch/sr15.

23. The author is indebted to Larry Birenbaum, David Schwartz, and Andrew Verhalen for help in framing these alternative strategies.

24. Holly Jean Buck et. al., "Evaluating the Efficacy and Equity of Environmental Stopgap Measures," *Nature* 3 (2020): 499–504, https://www.nature.com/articles/s41893-020 -0497-6; for figure 3 source of data, see Jane C. S. Long and John G. Shepherd, "The Strategic Value of Geoengineering Research," *Global Environmental Change, Handbook of Global Environmental Pollution* 1 (2014): 757–70, https://doi.org/10.1007/978-94 -007-5784-4_24. See also Douglas MacMartin, Katherine Ricke, and David W. Keith, "Solar Geoengineering as Part of an Overall Strategy for Meeting the 1.5°C Paris Target," *Philosophical Transactions of the Royal Society A: Mathematical, Physical and Engineering Sciences* 376 (April 2018), https://doi.org/10.1098/rsta.2016.0454; and

Jesse L. Reynolds, "Solar Geoengineering to Reduce Climate Change: A Review of Governance Proposals," *Proceedings of the Royal Society A* 475, no. 2229 (2019), https://doi.org/10.1098/rspa.2019.0255.

25. The thesis of cost-effectiveness here leaves aside potential side effects. Alternative approaches to SCI include placing large mirrors or shades in Earth's orbit or brightening the surface of the planet at great expense. For space mirrors, see Olivia Borgue and Andreas M. Hein, "A Zero-Radiation Pressure Sunshade for Supporting Climate Change Mitigation," *arXiv* 2112 (December 2021), https://arxiv.org/pdf/2112.13652.pdf. On the dispersal of aerosols, see Heleen de Coninck et al., "Chapter 4: Strengthening and Implementing the Global Response," in *Special Report: Global Warming of 1.5°C* (Geneva: Intergovernmental Panel on Climate Change, 2018): 313–443, https://www.ipcc.ch/site/assets/uploads/sites/2/2019/05/SR15_Chapter4_Low_Res.pdf.

26. See "Global Effects of Mount Pinatubo," NASA Earth Observatory, accessed February 2, 2022, https://earthobservatory.nasa.gov/images/1510/global-effects-of-mount-pinatubo; and Stephen Self et al., *The Atmospheric Impact of the 1991 Mount Pinatubo Eruption* (Washington, DC: U.S. Geological Survey, 1999), https://pubs.usgs.gov/pinatubo/self.

27. Other proposed options include dispersal via high-altitude balloons and even artillery shells. See Alan Robock et al., "Benefits, Risks, and Costs of Stratospheric Geoengineering," *Geophysical Research Letters* 36, no. 19 (October 2009), https://doi.org/10.1029/2009GL039209.

28. In 2018, the IPCC estimated the cost of SAI, "not taking into account indirect and social costs, research and development and monitoring expenses," to be as low as $1 billion to $10 billion annually: see Heleen de Coninck et al., "Chapter 4," 348; for a more recent estimate of $18 billion per year, see Wake Smith, "The Cost of Stratospheric Aerosol Injection Through 2100," *Environmental Research Letters* 15, no. 114004 (2020), https://iopscience.iop.org/article/10.1088/1748-9326/aba7e7/pdf; on the total global cost of achieving net zero, see Mekala Krishnan et al., *The Economic Transformation: What Would Change in the Net-Zero Transition* (New York: McKinsey Sustainability, 2002), https://www.mckinsey.com/business-functions/sustainability/our-insights/the-economic-transformation-what-would-change-in-the-net-zero-transition.

29. According to a widely cited study, estimated global particulate matter (PM) emissions in 2010 were approximately 263.5 million metric tons, or 263.5 teragrams (Tg). This includes 111 Tg for PM10, 81 Tg for PM2.5, 71 Tg for PM1, 9.5 Tg for Black Carbon, and 33Tg of Organic Carbon (1 Tg = 1,000,000 metric tons; 263 Tg = 263,000,000 metric tons); for more, see Zbigniew Klimont et. al., "Global Anthropogenic Emissions of Particulate Matter Including Black Carbon," *Atmospheric Chemistry and Physics* 17 (2017): 8681–723, https://doi.org/10.5194/acp-17-8681-2017.

30. Ironically, while steps to decarbonize the global economy are essential, the associated reduction in particulate matter will negate some of this beneficial reflection effect. For more, see "1. Is the Climate Warming?," Climate Change: Evidence and Causes, The Royal Society, last updated March 2020, https://royalsociety.org/topics-policy/projects/climate-change-evidence-causes/question-1/#:~:text=Yes.,%2D1970s%20%5BFigure%201a%5D; and James Temple, "We're About to Kill a Massive, Accidental

Experiment in Reducing Global Warming," *MIT Technology Review*, January 22, 2018, https://www.technologyreview.com/2018/01/22/67402/were-about-to-kill-a-massive -accidental-experiment-in-halting-global-warming.

31. The relevant atmospheric process is known as boundary layer convection. It is the primary mechanism for the movement of heat, momentum, moisture, and pollutants between the surface of the earth and the lower atmosphere.

32. See "Marine Cloud Brightening," University of Washington, College of the Environment, accessed January 12, 2022, https://static1.squarespace.com/static /5bbac81c7788975063632c65/t/5f98787d45584410048ad5c6/1603827838603 /MCB-FactSheet.pdf. A third atmospheric approach to reducing the warming effect of sunlight on Earth is cirrus cloud thinning (CCT). Unlike SAI and MCB, this would involve not enhancing the planet's reflectivity but reducing the amount of solar radiation trapped by these high-altitude clouds, allowing it to escape the atmosphere. This report does not address ground-level solar radiation management techniques. See Mark G. Lawrence et al., "Evaluating Climate Geoengineering Proposals in the Context of the Paris Agreement Temperature Goals," *Nature Communications* 9, no. 3734 (2018), https://www.nature.com/articles/s41467-018-05938-3.

33. It could also be used more locally, for example, to help cool the oceans above coral reefs. See Hannah M. Horowitz et al., "Effects of Sea Salt Aerosol Emissions for Marine Cloud Brightening on Atmospheric Chemistry: Implications for Radiative Forcing," *Geophysical Research Letters* 47, no. 4 (2020), https://agupubs.onlinelibrary .wiley.com/doi/10.1029/2019GL085838; Camilla W. Stjern et al., "Response to Marine Cloud Brightening in a Multi-Model Ensemble," *Atmospheric Chemistry and Physics* 18 (2018): 621–34, https://acp.copernicus.org/articles/18/621/2018/acp-18 -621-2018.pdf; and John Latham et al., "Marine Cloud Brightening," *Philosophical Transactions of the Royal Society A: Mathematical, Physical and Engineering* 370 (2012): 4217–62, https://doi.org/10.1098/rsta.2012.0086.

34. See Laurie Goering, "Sweden Rejects Pioneering Test of Solar Geoengineering Tech," Reuters, last updated March 31, 2021, https://www.reuters.com/article/us-climate -change-geoengineering-sweden/sweden-rejects-pioneering-test-of-solar-geoengineering -tech-idUSKBN2BN35X; and "SCoPEx," Keutsch Group at Harvard, accessed January 12, 2022, https://www.keutschgroup.com/scopex. A 2009 Russian experiment injected aerosols into the middle of the troposphere. See U.S. Government Accountability Office, *Climate Change: A Coordinated Strategy Could Focus Federal Geoengineering Research and Inform Governance Efforts*, GAO-10-903 (Washington, DC: U.S. Government Accountability Office, 2015), https://www.gao.gov/assets/gao-10-903.pdf.

35. See "Scientists Trial World-First 'Cloud Brightening' Technique to Protect Corals," Southern Cross University, April 17, 2020, https://www.scu.edu.au/engage/news/latest -news/2020/scientists-trial-world-first-cloud-brightening-technique-to-protect-corals .php; Jeff Tollefson, "Can Artificially Altered Clouds Save the Great Barrier Reef?," *Nature*, August 25, 2021, https://www.nature.com/articles/d41586-021-02290-3; Kerryn Bren et al., "Putting the Great Barrier Reef Marine Cloud Brightening Experiment Into Context," *Carnegie Climate Governance Initiative* (blog), May 13, 2020, https://www .c2g2.net/putting-the-great-barrier-reef-marine-cloud-brightening-experiment-into -context; and Graham Readfearn "Scientists Trial Cloud Brightening Equipment."

36. See "About Us," Marine Cloud Brightening Project, accessed February 16, 2022, https://mcbproject.org/about-us.

37. For a concise summary, see Alan Robock, "20 Reasons Why Geoengineering May Be a Bad Idea," *Bulletin of Atomic Scientists* 64, no. 2 (May/June 2008): 14–18, 59, https://climate.envsci.rutgers.edu/pdf/20Reasons.pdf.

38. See John Brockman, "We Are as Gods and Have to Get Good at It: Stewart Brand Talks About His Ecopragmatist Manifesto, A Talk with Stewart Brand," Edge, August 18, 2009, https://www.edge.org/conversation/stewart_brand-we-are-as-gods-and-have-to-get-good-at-it.

39. See Stephen M. Gardiner, "Climate Engineering," in *Ethics and the Contemporary World* (London: Routledge, 2019); and Stephen M. Gardiner, "Is 'Arming the Future' With Geoengineering Really the Lesser Evil? Some Doubts About the Ethics of Intentionally Manipulating the Climate System," in *Climate Ethics: Essential Readings*, ed. Stephen M. Gardiner, Simon Caney, Dale Jamieson, and Henry Sue (New York: Oxford University Press, 2010): 288.

40. See Elizabeth Chalecki, "When Considering Geopolitical Risks of Geoengineering, Don't Assume the Future Will Look Like the Past," *Internationalist* (blog), May 18, 2021, https://www.cfr.org/blog/when-assessing-geopolitical-risks-geoengineering-dont-assume-future-will-look-past.

41. See the CAN-International statement denouncing solar radiation modification and calling for a ban on its field research and deployment: Climate Action Network, *Position on Solar Radiation Modification* (Bonn, Germany: Climate Action Network International, 2019), https://climatenetwork.org/wp-content/uploads/2019/09/CAN-SRM-position.pdf. The Environmental Defense Fund has endorsed SCI research as the scale and speed of the climate crisis have grown and accelerated. Also see Jinnah and Nicholson, "The Hidden Politics of Climate Engineering."

42. For some examples, see Catriona McKinnon, "Sleepwalking Into Lock-in? Avoiding Wrongs to Future People in the Governance of Solar Radiation Management Research," *Environmental Politics* 28, no. 3 (2019), https://www.tandfonline.com/doi/abs/10.1080/09644016.2018.1450344; Jennie C. Stephens and Kevin Surprise, "The Hidden Injustices of Advancing Solar Geoengineering Research," *Global Sustainability* 3 (2020): 1–6, https://www.cambridge.org/core/services/aop-cambridge-core/content/view/F61C5DCBCA02E18F66CAC7E45CC76C57/S2059479819000280a.pdf/hidden_injustices_of_advancing_solar_geoengineering_research.pdf; and Jennie C. Stephens et al., "The Risks of Solar Geoengineering Research," *Science* 372, no. 6547 (June 2021): 1161, https://www.science.org/doi/10.1126/science.abj3679.

43. See "We Call for an International Non-Use Agreement on Solar Geoengineering," Solar Geoengineering Non-Use Agreement, accessed February 17, 2022, https://www.solargeoeng.org/non-use-agreement/open-letter; and Frank Biermann, et al., "Solar Geoengineering: The Case for an International Non-Use Agreement," *WIREs Climate Change* e754 (2022), https://doi.org/10.1002/wcc.754.

44. See Frank Biermann et al., "Solar Geoengineering."

45. For a concise and devastating critique of this proposal, see Holly Jean Buck, Twitter thread, January 17–19, 2022, https://twitter.com/hollyjeanbuck/status/1483898133599899654.

46.	According to the Working Group I's latest IPCC report, solar radiation management "has the potential to offset some effect of increasing GHGs on global and regional climate (high confidence), but there would be substantial residual or overcompensating climate change at the regional scale and seasonal timescale." See Richard P. Allan et al., *Climate Change 2021: The Physical Science Basis: Working Group I Contribution to the Sixth Assessment Report of the Intergovernmental Panel on Climate Change* (Intergovernmental Panel on Climate Change: Geneva, 2021), 4–90, https://www.ipcc.ch/report/ar6/wg1/downloads/report/IPCC_AR6_WGI_Full_Report.pdf; and William J. Broad, "How to Cool a Planet (Maybe)," *New York Times*, June 27, 2006, https://www.nytimes.com/2006/06/27/science/earth/27cool.html.

47.	See Edward A. Parson, "Geoengineering: Symmetric Precaution," *Science* 374, no. 6569 (November 2021), https://www.science.org/doi/pdf/10.1126/science.abm8462.

48.	See Rose C. Cairns, "Climate Geoengineering: Issues of Path-Dependence and Socio-Technical Lock-in," *WIREs Climate Change* 5, no. 5 (2014): 649–61, https://wires.onlinelibrary.wiley.com/doi/10.1002/wcc.296; Frank Biermann, "It Is Dangerous to Normalize Solar Geoengineering Research," *Nature*, June 29, 2021, https://www.nature.com/articles/d41586-021-01724-2; and Duncan McLaren and Olaf Corry, "The Politics and Governance of Research Into Solar Geoengineering," *WIREs Climate Change* 12, no. 3 (2021), https://doi.org/10.1002/wcc.707.

49.	See Daniel Bodansky and Andy Parker, "Research on Solar Climate Intervention Is the Best Defense Against Moral Hazard," *Issues in Science and Technology* 38, no. 1 (Fall 2021), https://issues.org/solar-climate-intervention-bodansky-parker-forum.

50.	See Susan Biniaz and Daniel Bodansky, *Solar Climate Intervention: Options for International Assessment and Decision-Making* (Arlington, VA: Center for Climate and Energy Solutions and SilverLining, 2020), https://www.c2es.org/wp-content/uploads/2020/07/solar-climate-intervention-options-for-international-assessment-and-decision-making.pdf.

51.	Gernot Wagner and Daniel Zizzamia, "Green Moral Hazards," *Ethics, Policy & Environment* (July 2021), https://gwagner.com/wp-content/uploads/Wagner-Zizzamia-EPE-2021-Green-Moral-Hazards.pdf.

52.	Aseem Mahajan, Dustin Tingley, and Gernot Wagner, "Fast, Cheap, and Imperfect? U.S. Public Opinion About Solar Geoengineering," *Environmental Politics* 28, no. 3 (May 2018), https://doi.org/10.1080/09644016.2018.1479101.

53.	For the most comprehensive survey of surveys to date, see Elizabeth T. Burns et al., "What Do People Think When They Think About Solar Geoengineering? A Review of Empirical Social Science Literature, and Prospects for Future Research," *Earth's Future* 4, no. 11 (November 2016), 536–42, https://agupubs.onlinelibrary.wiley.com/doi/10.1002/2016EF000461. See also Maura M. K. Austin and Benjamin A. Converse, "In Search of Weakened Resolve: Does Climate-Engineering Awareness Decrease Individuals' Commitment to Mitigation?," *Journal of Environmental Psychology* 78, no. 101690 (December 2021), https://doi.org/10.1016/j.jenvp.2021.101690; Christine Merk, Gert Pönitzsch, and Katrin Rehdanz, "Do Climate Engineering Experts Display Moral-Hazard Behaviour?," *Climate Policy* 19, no. 2 (2019): 231–43, https://doi.org/10.1080/14693062.2018.1494534; and Christine Merk, Gert Pönitzsch, and Katrin Rehdanz, "Knowledge About Aerosol Injection Does Not Reduce Individual Mitigation Efforts," *Environmental Research Letters* 11 (2016), http://dx.doi.org/10.1088/1748-9326/11/5/054009.

54. See Mark G. Lawrence and Paul J. Crutzen, "Was Breaking the Taboo on Research on Climate Engineering via Albedo Modification a Moral Hazard, or a Moral Imperative?," *Earth's Future* 5, no. 2 (2017): 136–43; and Gardiner, "Arming the Future."

55. See Joseph E. Aldy et al., "Social Science Research to Inform Solar Geoengineering," *Science* 374, no. 6569 (2021) 815–18, https://www.science.org/doi/10.1126/science.abj6517.

56. See Allan et al., *Climate Change 2021: The Physical Science Basis*, SPM-1–SPM-41; Intergovernmental Panel on Climate Change Working Group II, *Climate Change 2022: Impacts, Adaptation, and Vulnerability*; Intergovernmental Panel on Climate Change Working Group III, *Climate Change 2022: Mitigation of Climate Change*; and Stewart M. Patrick, "The Long-Awaited Climate Emergency Is Now," *World Politics Review*, August 16, 2021, https://www.worldpoliticsreview.com/articles/29889/even-with -mitigation-climate-change-will-remake-the-planet.

57. See Rob Picheta, "CO_2 Levels in the Atmosphere Reach a 3 Million-Year High, Putting the World 'Way Off Track' on Climate Goals," CNN, last updated October 25, 2021, https://www.cnn.com/2021/10/25/world/emissions-climate-greenhouse-gas-bulletin -wmo-intl/index.html?mc_cid=11bc3962d3&mc_eid=b66030a849; and "Understanding the Science of Ocean and Coastal Acidification," United States Environmental Protection Agency, last accessed April 13, 2022, https://www.epa.gov/ocean -acidification/understanding-science-ocean-and-coastal-acidification.

58. See "2021 One of the Seven Warmest Years on Record, WMO Consolidated Data Shows," World Meteorological Organization, January 19, 2022, https://public.wmo.int/en/media /press-release/2021-one-of-seven-warmest-years-record-wmo-consolidated-data-shows.

59. See "IPCC Report: 'Code Red' for Human Driven Global Heating, Warns UN Chief," *UN News: Global Perspective Human Stories, United Nations*, August 9, 2021, https:// news.un.org/en/story/2021/08/1097362.

60. See "The Growing Risk of Climate 'Tipping Points': Scientific Evidence and Policy Responses" (Council on Foreign Relations, virtual roundtable, February 4, 2022), https:// www.cfr.org/event/growing-risk-climate-tipping-points-scientific-evidence-and-policy -responses; Timothy M. Lenton et al., "Climate Tipping Points—Too Risky to Bet Against," *Nature*, corrected April 9, 2020, https://www.nature.com/articles/d41586-019-03595-0; and Stephen Leahy, "Climate Change Driving Entire Planet to Dangerous 'Tipping Point,'" *National Geographic*, November 27, 2019, https://www.nationalgeographic.com /science/article/earth-tipping-point.

61. See "The Growing Risk of Climate 'Tipping Points'"; and Sarah Kaplan, "A Critical Ocean System May Be Heading for Collapse Due to Climate Change, Study Finds," *Washington Post*, August 5, 2021, https://www.washingtonpost.com/climate-environment /2021/08/05/change-ocean-collapse-atlantic-meridional.

62. See International Panel on Climate Change Working Group II, *Climate Change 2022: Impacts, Adaptation, and Vulnerability*; and Stewart M. Patrick, "Climate Change Is Putting the SDGs Further Out of Reach," *World Politics Review*, August 23, 2021, https://www.worldpoliticsreview.com/articles/29907/absent-mitigation-climate-change -also-threatens-the-sdgs.

63. See National Intelligence Council, *National Intelligence Estimate: Climate Change and International Responses Increasing Challenges to U.S. National Security Through 2040*,

NIC-NIE-2021-10030-A (Washington, DC: National Intelligence Council, 2021), accessed January 12, 2022, https://www.dni.gov/files/ODNI/documents/assessments /NIE_Climate_Change_and_National_Security.pdf; and Stewart M. Patrick, "The U.S. Is Waking Up to Climate Change's Security Implications," *World Politics Review*, November 8, 2021, https://www.worldpoliticsreview.com/articles/30101/absent -mitigation-climate-change-will-have-major-security-implications.

64. On the importance of ethical inquiry, see Steve Rayner et al., "The Oxford Principles," *Climate Change* 121 (2013): 499–512, https://link.springer.com/content/pdf/10.1007 /s10584-012-0675-2.pdf; Stephen M. Gardiner and Augustin Fragnière, "The Tollgate Principles for the Governance of Geoengineering: Moving Beyond the Oxford Principles to an Ethically More Robust Approach," *Ethics, Policy & Environment* 21, no. 2 (2018): 143–74, https://doi.org/10.1080/21550085.2018.1509472; and National Academies of Sciences, Engineering, and Medicine, *Reflecting Sunlight: Recommendations for Solar Geoengineering Research and Research Governance* (Washington, DC: National Academies Press, 2021), https://doi.org/10.17226/25762.

65. According to the *Global Landscape of Climate Finance 2021* report, total climate finance reached $632 billion in 2019/2020. See Barbara Buchner, et al., *Global Landscape of Climate Finance 2021* (Washington, DC: Climate Policy Initiative, 2021): 2, https://www .climatepolicyinitiative.org/publication/global-landscape-of-climate-finance-2021.

66. See "Earth's Radiation Budget Program," National Oceanic and Atmospheric Administration, accessed January 12, 2021, https://csl.noaa.gov/research/erb/about.html.

67. The Office of Naval Research is obliged to report back to the House and Senate armed services committees on the capabilities that the Pentagon and the National Laboratories need to support this research. See *William M. (Mac) Thornberry National Defense Authorization Act for Fiscal Year 2021*, Public Law No: 116-283, *U.S. Statutes at Large* 116 (2021), https://www.congress.gov/116/bills/hr6395/BILLS-116hr6395enr.pdf.

68. This is an increase for NOAA from $9 million in FY 2021 and $4 million in FY 2020.

69. Based on conversations with NOAA and DOE officials.

70. The thirteen agencies include the Departments of Agriculture, Commerce, Defense, Energy, Health and Human Services, the Interior, State, and Transportation, as well as the EPA, NASA, NSF, Smithsonian Institution, and the U.S. Agency for International Development. The USGCRP runs the congressionally mandated quadrennial National Climate Assessment.

71. See U.S. Congress, House, *Consolidated Appropriations Act, 2022*, H.R. 2471, 117th Cong. 2nd sess., *Congressional Record*, https://www.congress.gov/117/bills/hr2471 /BILLS-117hr2471enr.pdf.

72. See "New Report Says U.S. Should Cautiously Pursue Solar Geoengineering Research to Better Understand Options for Responding to Climate Change Risks," National Academies of Sciences, Engineering, and Medicine (news release), March 25, 2021, https://www.nationalacademies.org/news/2021/03/new-report-says-u-s-should -cautiously-pursue-solar-geoengineering-research-to-better-understand-options-for- responding-to-climate-change-risks; and Jeff Tollefson, "U.S. Urged to Invest in Sun-Dimming Studies as Climate Warms," *Nature*, March 29, 2021, https://www.nature.com /articles/d41586-021-00822-5.

73. See Daniel Bodansky, "Customary (And Not So Customary) International Environmental Law, *Indiana Journal of Global Legal Studies* 3, no. 1 (Fall 1995): 105–19, https://www.repository.law.indiana.edu/cgi/viewcontent.cgi?article=1060&context=ijgls; Mara Tignino and Christian Bréthaut, "The Role of International Case Law in Implementing the Obligation Not to Cause Significant Harm," *International Environmental Agreements: Politics, Law and Economics* 20 (2020): 631–48, https://link.springer.com/article/10.1007/s10784-020-09503-6; and Neil Craik, "The Duty to Cooperate in the Customary Law of Environmental Impact Assessment," *International & Comparative Law Quarterly* 69, no. 1 (January 2020): 239–59, https://www.cambridge.org/core/journals/international-and-comparative-law-quarterly/article/abs/duty-to-cooperate-in-the-customary-law-of-environmental-impact-assessment/AB1F146A96DB6DAE9B38DE669E20ADCE.

74. See Jesse Reynolds, "The International Regulation of Climate Engineering: Lessons from Nuclear Power," *Journal of Environmental Law* 26 (2014): 269–89, https://jreynolds.org/wp-content/uploads/2017/09/Reynolds-2014-The-International-Regulation-of-Climate-Engineering-Lessons-from-Nuclear-Power.pdf; and Reynolds, *The Governance of Solar Geoengineering*.

75. See Florian Rabitz, "Gene Drives and the International Biodiversity Regime," *Review of European, Comparative & International Environmental Law* 28, no. 3 (2019): 339–48, https://doi.org/10.1111/reel.12289; Delphine Thizy, Isabelle Coche, and Jantina de Vries, "Providing a Policy Framework for Responsible Gene Drive Research," *Wellcome Open Research* 5, no. 173 (2020), https://www.ncbi.nlm.nih.gov/pmc/articles/PMC7477640/pdf/wellcomeopenres-5-17577.pdf; and Ewen Callaway, "UN Treaty Agrees to Limit Gene Drives but Rejects a Moratorium," *Nature*, corrected November 30, 2018, https://www.nature.com/articles/d41586-018-07600-w.

76. The purpose of the envisioned report was to establish criteria to define "sunlight reflection"; assess the scientific state of play and identify the leading actors in the field; summarize the potential risks, benefits, and uncertainties of such interventions; and consider what future "global governance frameworks" could be appropriate for regulating this emerging suite of technologies, including avoiding the dangers of unilateral action. The eleven countries joining Switzerland in this resolution were Burkina Faso, the Federated States of Micronesia, Georgia, Liechtenstein, Mali, Monaco, Montenegro, New Zealand, Niger, the Republic of Korea, and Senegal. See UN Environment Assembly Resolution for Consideration, *Geoengineering and Its Governance*, February 21, 2019, available from https://s3.documentcloud.org/documents/5750122/Draft-resolution-on-geoengineering-for.pdf.

77. See Jean Chemnick, "U.S. Blocks UN Resolution on Geoengineering," *E&E News*, March 15, 2019, https://www.scientificamerican.com/article/u-s-blocks-u-n-resolution-on-geoengineering; Jinnah and Nicholson, "The Hidden Politics of Climate Engineering"; and Jesse Reynolds, "Perspectives on the UNEA Resolution," *Harvard's Solar Geoengineering Research Program* (blog), March 29, 2019, https://geoengineering.environment.harvard.edu/blog/perspectives-unea-resolution#JesseReynolds.

78. See Gernot Wagner and Martin L. Weitzman, "Playing God," *Foreign Policy*, October 24, 2012, https://foreignpolicy.com/2012/10/24/playing-god. For a skeptical take on the relevance of the free-driver concept, see Stephen Gardiner's debate with David Morrow in the following articles: Stephen Gardiner, "Why 'Global Public Good' Is a Treacherous Term, Especially for Geoengineering," *Climatic Change* 123, no. 2 (March 2014): 101–06, https://www.proquest.com/docview/1504829455; and David R. Morrow, "Why

Geoengineering Is a Public Good, Even If It Is Bad," *Climatic Change* 123, no. 2 (March 2014): 95–100, https://link.springer.com/article/10.1007/s10584-013-0967-1.

79. See National Intelligence Council, *National Intelligence Estimate: Climate Change.*

80. See Sarah Fecht, "We Need Laws on Geoengineering," *State of the Planet*, March 20, 2018, https://news.climate.columbia.edu/2018/03/20/geoengineering-climate-law-book.

81. See Elizabeth Chalecki, "When Considering Geopolitical Risks of Geoengineering."

82. See Stephen M. Gardiner, "The Desperation Argument for Geoengineering," *PS: Political Science & Politics* 46, no.1 (2013): 28–33, https://www.cambridge.org/core/journals/ps-political-science-and-politics/article/abs/desperation-argument-for-geoengineering/23D9326AEA5756D07C05DA7B24140A86.

83. See Edward A. Parson and Lia N. Ernst, "International Governance of Climate Engineering," *Theoretical Inquiries in Law* 14, no. 1 (2013): 307–37, www7.tau.ac.il/ojs/index.php/til/article/download/871/828; and Edward A. Parson and Jesse L. Reynolds, "Solar Geoengineering Governance: Insights From a Scenario Exercise," *Futures* 132 (September 2021), https://doi.org/10.1016/j.futures.2021.102805.

84. Some analysts (and fiction writers) have suggested that nonstate actors, including multibillionaires, might launch private sunlight reflection efforts of their own. Such a "Greenfinger" scenario (as David Victor has christened it) seems implausible, given the infrastructure requirements of delivering millions of tons of material into the stratosphere on an ongoing basis and the ability of powerful sovereign states to detect and interdict SCI efforts of which they had not approved. Any such effort would presumably require the support or at least acquiescence of a host state vulnerable to targeting. See David G. Victor, "On the Regulation of Geoengineering," *Oxford Review of Economic Policy* 24, no. 2 (Summer 2008): 322–36, https://www.jstor.org/stable/23606647.

85. On China's recent interest in weather modification, see Helen Davidson, "China 'Modified' the Weather to Create Clear Skies for Political Celebration–Study," *Guardian*, December 5, 2021, https://www.theguardian.com/world/2021/dec/06/china-modified-the-weather-to-create-clear-skies-for-political-celebration-study.

86. See James Temple, "China Builds One of the World's Largest Geoengineering Research Programs," *MIT Technology Review*, August 2, 2017, https://www.technologyreview.com/2017/08/02/4291/china-builds-one-of-the-worlds-largest-geoengineering-research-programs. See Lili Pike, "Solar Geoengineering Rises in the East," China Dialogue, July 13, 2018, https://chinadialogue.net/en/climate/10733-solar-geoengineering-rises-in-the-east.

87. See U.S. Department of State, "U.S.-China Joint Glasgow Declaration on Enhancing Climate Action in the 2020s," media note, November 10, 2021, https://www.state.gov/u-s-china-joint-glasgow-declaration-on-enhancing-climate-action-in-the-2020s.

88. See Biniaz and Bodansky, *Solar Climate Intervention.* Parson and Ernst identify three distinct functions for institutions to ideally serve in this space: research and assessment, deployment decisions and regulatory oversight, and management and response to security threats. See Parson and Ernst, "International Governance of Climate Engineering," 331.

89. The latest quadrennial report of the Montreal Protocol's scientific assessment panel, due out later this year, will include the first significant analysis of the potential effects of SAI on the ozone layer.

90. In February 2022, the sixth assessment report of IPCC Working Group II included a single paragraph on sunlight reflection in its lengthy summary for policymakers. See Hans-O. Pörtner et al., "Summary for Policymakers," in *Climate Change 2022: Impacts, Adaptation, and Vulnerability* (Geneva: Intergovernmental Panel on Climate Change), https://report.ipcc.ch/ar6wg2/pdf/IPCC_AR6_WGII_SummaryForPolicymakers.pdf.

91. See Janos Pasztor, "The Climate Conversation No One Wants to Have," *Foreign Policy*, January 17, 2022, https://foreignpolicy.com/2022/01/17/climate-change-solar -geoengineering-radiation-modification-governance.

92. Marlon Hourdequin, "Climate Change, Climate Engineering, and the 'Global Poor': What Does Justice Require?" *Ethics, Policy and Environment* 21, no. 3 (2018): 270–88, https://www.tandfonline.com/doi/full/10.1080/21550085.2018.1562525.

93. See Simon Nicholson, Sikina Jinnah, and Alexander Gillespie, "Solar Radiation Management: A Proposal for Immediate Polycentric Governance," *Climate Policy* 18, no. 3 (2018): 322–34, https://doi.org/10.1080/14693062.2017.1400944. For an elaboration on these alternative approaches to multilateral cooperation, see Stewart M. Patrick, "The Four Contending Approaches to Multilateralism Under Biden," *World Politics Review*, May 24, 2021, https://www.worldpoliticsreview.com/articles/29675 /on-foreign-policy-us-mulls-what-comes-after-the-liberal-international-order.

94. This is hardly a new suggestion. See Daniel Bodansky and Kelly Wanser, *Think Globally, Govern Locally: Designing a National Research Program on Near-Term Climate Risks and Possible Intervention* (Arlington, VA: Center for Climate and Energy Solutions and Silver-Lining, 2021), https://www.c2es.org/wp-content/uploads/2021/04/Think-Globally -Govern-Locally-Designing-a-National-Research-Program.pdf; and Bipartisan Policy Center, *Task Force on Climate Remediation Research* (Washington, DC: Bipartisan Policy Center, 2011), https://bipartisanpolicy.org/download/?file=/wp-content/uploads/2019 /03/BPC-Climate-Remediation-Final-Report.pdf.

95. See *Consolidated Appropriations Act, 2022*.

96. See Daniel Bodansky and Susan Biniaz, *Climate Intervention: The Case for Research* (Arlington, VA: Center for Climate and Energy Solutions and SilverLining, 2020), https://www.silverlining.ngo/case-for-research-paper.

97. Influential efforts to define this ethical terrain include the Oxford Principles and the Tollgate Principles. See Rayner et al., "The Oxford Principles"; and Gardiner and Fragnière, "The Tollgate Principles." On adopting a symmetrical approach to precaution, see Edward A. Parson, "Geoengineering: Symmetric Precaution," *Science* 374, no. 6569 (2021): 795, https://www.science.org/doi/10.1126/science.abm8462.

98. The Atmospheric Climate Intervention Research Act was first introduced by Representative Jerry McNerney (D-CA) in 2019. See U.S. Congress, House, *Atmospheric Climate Intervention Research Act of 2019*, HR 5519, 116th Congress, 1st sess., December 19, 2019, https://www.congress.gov/bill/116th-congress/house-bill/5519.

99. See Joseph A. Aldy et. al., "Social Science Research to Inform Solar Geoengineering," *Science* 374, no. 6569 (November 2021). 815–18, https://www.science.org/doi/10.1126 /science.abj6517.

100. This determination is based on one-on-one conversations with U.S. government officials in relevant agencies.

101. In FY 2021, these agencies were allocated $3.27 billion for the stated purposes. See "Budget: Fiscal Year (FY) 2022 USGCRP Budget Crosscut by Agency," About USGCRP, GlobalChange.gov, accessed February 18, 2022, https://www.globalchange .gov/about/budget.

102. See Office of Chief Financial Officer, *Department of Energy FY 2022 Congressional Budget Request: Science*, DOE/CF-0175 Volume 4 (Washington, DC: Department of Energy, 2021), 7, https://www.energy.gov/sites/default/files/2021-06/doe-fy2022 -budget-volume-4-v5.pdf; and *Consolidated Appropriations Act, 2022.*

103. See "Breaking Down the Infrastructure Bill's Impact on Climate Change," *PBS News Hour* video, 5:15, August 5, 2021, https://www.pbs.org/newshour/show/breaking-down-the -infrastructure-bills-impact-on-climate-change; and U.S. Department of Defense, "The Department of Defense Releases President's Fiscal Year 2022 Defense Budget," news release, May 28, 2021, https://www.defense.gov/News/Releases/Release/Article/2638711 /the-department-of-defense-releases-the-presidents-fiscal-year-2022-defense-budg.

104. This is based on extensive conversations with Silicon Valley entrepreneurs and venture capitalists involved in climate-related investments. If the private sector will play any role in sunlight reflection research and development, it will likely be limited to tenders for public procurement contracts.

105. For elaboration of the potential role of nonstate actors (including universities) in the governance of solar climate intervention research, see Jesse L. Reynolds and Edward A. Parson, "Nonstate Governance of Solar Geoengineering Research," *Climatic Change* 160 (2020): 323–42, https://doi.org/10.1007/s10584-020-02702-9; and Jane Long and Edward (Ted) A. Parson, "Functions of Geoengineering Research Governance," *UCLA School of Law, Public Law Research Paper*, no. 19-42 (2019), http://dx.doi.org /10.2139/ssrn.3476376.

106. See Bodansky and Wanser, *Think Globally, Govern Locally.*

107. See Paul Voosen, "U.S. Needs Solar Geoengineering Research Program, National Academies Says," *Science*, March 25, 2021, https://www.science.org/content/article /us-needs-solar-geoengineering-research-program-national-academies-says.

108. See Edward A. Parson and David W. Keith, "End the Deadlock on Governance of Geoengineering Research," *Science* 339, no. 6125 (2013): 1278–79, https://www .science.org/doi/abs/10.1126/science.1232527.

109. That act "defines weather modification as any activity performed with the intention of producing artificial changes in the composition, behavior, or dynamics of that atmosphere." See Bodansky and Wanser, *Think Globally, Govern Locally*, 9.

110. See Parson and Keith, "End the Deadlock on Governance of Geoengineering Research"; Gernot Wagner, "Research Governance," in *Geoengineering: The Gamble* (Cambridge, UK: Polity Press, 2021).

111. Such an outcome would be consistent with the Oxford Principles, a set of proposed guidelines formulated in 2009 that among other things call for research on sunlight reflection to be treated and governed as a global public good. See Steve Rayner, Tim Kruger, and Julian Savulescu, *The Regulation of Geoengineering* (London, UK: House of Commons Science and Technology Committee, session 2009-10), 5, http://www .geoengineering.ox.ac.uk/publications.parliament.uk/pa/cm200910/cmselect/cmsctech /221/221.pdf.

112. See Bodansky and Wanser, *Think Globally, Govern Locally.*

113. CERN is the world's largest particle physics laboratory, jointly operated by twenty-three member states. The ISS, a multinational project involving the space agencies of the United States, Canada, Japan, Russia, and the European Union that has provided a platform for research collaboration among Western nations and Russia.

114. See "SRMGI Becomes the Degrees Initiative," Degrees Initiative, November 10, 2021, https://www.srmgi.org/2021/11/10/srmgi-becomes-the-degrees-initiative-2; and "Putting Developing Countries at the Centre of the SRM Conversation," Degrees Initiative, accessed January 13, 2022, https://www.srmgi.org.

115. See Bodansky and Wanser, *Think Globally, Govern Locally.*

116. On the potential for a U.S. research program to serve as a model for other countries and allow them to participate in SCI governance, see comments from NASEM report committee member Ambuj Sagar, in "Setting an Agenda for Solar Geoengineering Research and Governance," Woodrow Wilson International Center for Scholars, May 6, 2021, https://www.wilsoncenter.org/event/setting-agenda-solar-geoengineering -research-and-governance.

117. See Biniaz and Bodansky, *Solar Climate Intervention.*

118. See Nicholson, Jinnah, and Gillespie, "Solar Radiation Management: A Proposal for Immediate Polycentric Governance."

119. In November 2021, the Paris Peace Forum launched a Global Commission on Governing Risks from Climate Overshoot, which will consider sunlight reflection as one policy response. (The author was a member of the forum's steering committee, which proposed such a commission.) Edward Parson has also called for a "World Commission on Climate Engineering." See Edward A. Parson, *Starting the Dialogue on Climate Engineering Governance: A World Commission*, Fixing Climate Governance Series Policy Brief no. 8 (Waterloo, ON, Canada: Centre for International Governance Innovation, 2017), https://www.cigionline.org/static/documents/documents/Fixing%20Climate%20 Governance%20PB%20no8_0.pdf.

120. See World Commission on Environment and Development, *Our Common Future* (New York: United Nations, 1987), https://sustainabledevelopment.un.org/content /documents/5987our-common-future.pdf; International Commission on Intervention and State Sovereignty, *The Responsibility to Protect* (Ottawa, ON, Canada: International Development Research Centre, 2001), https://www.globalr2p.org/resources/the -responsibility-to-protect-report-of-the-international-commission-on-intervention -and-state-sovereignty-2001.

121. See Richard Gowan and Pyotr Kurzin, "The UN Security Council Finally Considers Weighing in on Climate Security," *World Politics Review*, November 29, 2021, https:// www.worldpoliticsreview.com/articles/30148/climate-security-might-be-a-victim-of -great-power-un-diplomacy.

122. See Jesse Reynolds, "Linking Solar Geoengineering and Emissions Reductions: Strategically Resolving an International Climate Change Policy Dilemma," *Climate Policy* (2021): 1–16, https://doi.org/10.1080/14693062.2021.1993125; and Edward A. Parson, "Climate Engineering in Global Climate Governance: Implications for

Participation and Linkage," *Transnational Environmental Law* 3, no.1 (2014): 89–110, https://doi.org/10.1017/S2047102513000496.

123.   See John Virgoe, "International Governance of a Possible Geoengineering Intervention to Combat Climate Change," *Climactic Change* 95 (2009): 103–19, https://doi.org/10.1007/s10584-008-9523-9.

ABOUT THE AUTHOR

Stewart M. Patrick is the James H. Binger senior fellow in global governance and director of the International Institutions and Global Governance program at the Council on Foreign Relations. His areas of expertise include multilateral cooperation on global issues; U.S. policy toward international institutions, including the United Nations; and the challenges posed by fragile and post-conflict states. Patrick is a life member of the Council on Foreign Relations and served on the Paris Peace Forum's international steering group on the governance of solar geoengineering.

Before joining CFR, Patrick was a fellow at the Center for Global Development, where he directed the center's research and policy engagement on the intersection between security and development. Previously, he served on the secretary of state's policy planning staff, with lead staff responsibility for U.S. policy toward Afghanistan and a range of global and transnational issues. Patrick is the author of *The Sovereignty Wars: Reconciling America with the World*, as well as *Weak Links: Fragile States, Global Threats, and International Security* and *The Best Laid Plans: The Origins of American Multilateralism and the Dawn of the Cold War*. He is a coauthor of the 2020 CFR Task Force Report, *Improving Pandemic Preparedness: Lessons from COVID-19*. A frequent media commentator, he has written several hundred articles and opinion pieces on international cooperation. He writes a regular column for *World Politics Review*, as well as the CFR blog *The Internationalist*. Patrick received his bachelor's degree in human biology from Stanford University and two master's degrees, as well as a doctorate in international relations, from Oxford University, where he was a Rhodes Scholar.

ADVISORY COMMITTEE
Reflecting Sunlight to Reduce Climate Risk

Jesse H. Ausubel
Rockefeller University

Daniel Bodansky
Arizona State University

Elizabeth L. Chalecki
University of Nebraska Omaha

Chloe Demrovsky
*Disaster Recovery Institute
International*

Sarah J. Doherty
University of Washington

David P. Fidler, *ex officio*
Council on Foreign Relations

Stephen M. Gardiner
University of Washington

Michael Gerrard
Columbia Law School

Sherri W. Goodman, *chair*
*Woodrow Wilson International
Center for Scholars*

Alice C. Hill, *ex officio*
Council on Foreign Relations

Joshua Horton
Harvard University

Sikina Jinnah
*University of California,
Santa Cruz*

Miles Kahler, *ex officio*
Council on Foreign Relations

Douglas MacMartin
Cornell University

Simon Nicholson
American University

Andrew R. Parker
The Degrees Initiative

Edward A. Parson
UCLA School of Law

Janos Pasztor
*Carnegie Climate Governance
Initiative*

This report reflects the judgments and recommendations of the authors. It does not nec-essarily represent the views of members of the advisory committee, whose involvement should in no way be interpreted as an endorsement of the report by either themselves or the organizations with which they are affiliated.

Kilaparti Ramakrishna
Woods Hole Oceanographic Institution

Jesse Reynolds
UCLA School of Law

Theodore Roosevelt IV
Barclays

Chris Sacca
Lowercarbon Capital

Jonathan M. Silver
Guggenheim Partners

Gernot Wagner
New York University

Kelly Wanser
SilverLining

MISSION STATEMENT OF THE INTERNATIONAL INSTITUTIONS AND GLOBAL GOVERNANCE PROGRAM

The International Institutions and Global Governance (IIGG) program at the Council on Foreign Relations is supported by a generous grant from the Robina Foundation. It aims to identify the institutional requirements for effective multilateral cooperation in the twenty-first century. The program is motivated by the recognition that the architecture of global governance—largely reflecting the world as it existed in 1945—has not kept pace with fundamental changes in the international system. These shifts include the spread of transnational challenges, the rise of new powers, and the mounting influence of nonstate actors. Existing multilateral arrangements thus provide an inadequate foundation for addressing many of today's most pressing threats and for advancing U.S. national and broader global interests. Given these trends, U.S. policymakers and other interested actors require rigorous, independent analysis of current structures of multilateral cooperation, and of the promises and pitfalls of alternative international arrangements. The IIGG program meets these needs by analyzing the strengths and weaknesses of existing multilateral institutions and proposing reforms tailored to new international circumstances.